a new spin on DRUNKARD'S PATH

12 Innovative Projects

DECEPTIVELY SIMPLE TECHNIQUES

John Kubiniec

C&T PUBLISHING

Publisher: Amy Marson

Creative Director: Gailen Runge

Editors: Lynn Koolish and Monica Gyulai

Technical Editors: Debbie Rodgers and Gailen Runge

Cover/Book Designer: April Mostek

Production Coordinator: Tim Manibusan

Production Editors: Jessica Brotman, Jennifer Warren, and Nicole Rolandelli

Illustrator: Jessica Zimmerman

Photo Assistant: Carly Jean Marin

Instructional photography by Diane Pedersen, unless otherwise noted

Published by C&T Publishing, Inc., P.O. Box 1456, Lafayette, CA 94549

Library of Congress Cataloging-in-Publication Data

Names: Kubiniec, John, 1957- author.

Title: A new spin on drunkard's path : 12 innovative projects - deceptively simple techniques / John Kubiniec.

Description: Lafayette, CA : C&T Publishing, 2016.

Identifiers: LCCN 2015049435 | ISBN 9781617453014 (soft cover)

Subjects: LCSH: Patchwork--Patterns. | Quilting--Patterns. | Drunkard's path quilts.

Classification: LCC TT835 .K825 2016 | DDC 746.46--dc23

LC record available at http://lccn.loc.gov/2015049435

Printed in China

10 9 8 7 6 5 4 3 2 1

Dedication

To all of my students who are willing to explore, create, and ask the question: "What would happen if ... ?"

Acknowledgments

To Joanna Rose, for her generosity in creating the show *Infinite Variety: Three Centuries of Red and White Quilts*.

To everyone at *McCall's Quilting* who helped get this all started and kept it going.

To everyone at BERNINA of America, Inc. for their support and the use of the BERNINA 750 QE, as well as to Linda Fellows and her staff at The Bobbin Case in Rochester, New York.

A special thank-you to the following companies who supplied fabric for the projects in this book:

- Clothworks—Joyce Cronkhite
- Michael Miller Fabrics—Christine Osmers
- RJR Fabrics—Demetria Hayward
- Studio E Fabrics—Scott Fortonoff and Linda Galvin
- Windham Fabrics—Laura Jaquinto, Nell Timmer, and Crystal Nilpilrom

To Marti and Richard Michell for their support and for their wonderful products.

To Donna Lamb and the staff at Quilting by the Lake for providing a place to learn and explore ideas—schweinfurthartcenter.org.

To everyone at C&T Publishing who worked on this project, thanks for all your support and encouragement.

Finally, to Ray Pool, for his support and encouragement over the years and throughout this project, and especially for supplying food and drink at critical moments.

CONTENTS

PREFACE

The idea for this book was sparked in 2011 by the New York exhibition *Infinite Variety: Three Centuries of Red and White Quilts*. Held at the Park Avenue Armory, a grand building that dates from the Gilded Age, the exhibition featured more than 600 quilts from the collection of Joanna Rose. A sense of excitement and expectation led up to the show, and I was lucky to be there when the doors opened. We gasped when we glimpsed at what was to come!

Sheer magic—the view as the doors opened at the Park Avenue Armory

We entered a massive space that had been transformed into a cathedral of quilts. I was so captivated that I spent the entire day taking in the array and later returned to the show several times. One day while staring at a quilt, I realized that what appeared to be circles were actually Drunkard's Path blocks arranged to look like red circles floating on a white background.

Drunkard's Path blocks arranged to look like circles

My mind started to race ... What else could you do to change the block up a bit? My answer came at 3 A.M., when I woke with a vision of a Drunkard's Path block with a half-square triangle in the corner. I sketched it out on a nearby envelope, and in the morning I drafted the block and began to play around with it. The result was my quilt *Infinite Possibilities*, which appeared in the March/April 2013 issue of *McCall's Quilting*.

McCall's Quilting, March/April 2013

I thought I had come up with something brand-new, but this variation has been around for a long time. I soon found other variations of the block and began to figure out easier ways to construct them. I continued to play with the blocks, and from those experiments, combined with the efforts of my students, this book was born.

Play! Create! Enjoy!

introduction

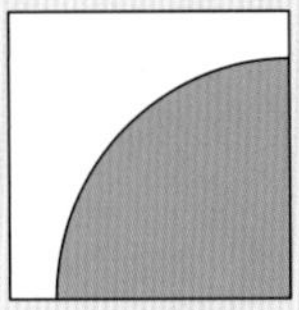

All of the quilts in this book are built on variations of the Drunkard's Path block. Some have been around for a long time, and to those I am merely applying modern cutting and piecing techniques. Others have been created and developed by my students as we have played with this versatile block.

At first glance, a quilt might look very complex and difficult, but I break down the steps into building blocks. You will be instructed to sew together traditional block units and then trim them using templates. This approach enables you to make complex-looking blocks involving many pieces and curves with relative ease.

If you detest curved piecing, I hope these patterns will entice you to give it a try and that my techniques will help you conquer your fears. If you already love curved piecing, the variations and patterns will help you explore new design possibilities.

Quilters near and far have struggled to sew curves. You may have even tried and screamed, "Never again!" I am here to say, "Never say never."

The second quilt I ever made included 3″ Drunkard's Path blocks. They were bears to make, and the small size didn't help. I wasn't sure I would ever sew curves again.

But over time I did more curved piecing, and somewhere along the way my fear of curves turned into a love of curves. When I start a class, I tell my students that curved piecing is easy. I immediately get those looks—students watching with disbelief over the tops of their eyeglasses. When I say, "I only use three pins," I get more looks, accompanied with muttering. But I turn the doubtful into believers, as I hope to do here with this book.

So come and explore curved piecing; make the block variations. Play around with these variations, make a few blocks for practice, throw them up on a design wall, and see what you can create. You will hone your curved-piecing skills and also get your mind thinking about what you might do. Feel free to adapt the patterns, swap out one variation for another, and combine multiple variations in a quilt. Have fun, play, and always ask yourself: "What would happen if…?"

tools OF THE TRADE

The right tools make it easier to do good work. In addition to basic sewing tools, here are some tools I found especially helpful when giving the Drunkard's Path block a new spin.

Rotary Cutters

A good rotary cutter with a sharp blade is a must when working with templates. You can easily cut through 4–6 layers of fabric at once with a good, sharp blade. A 45 mm rotary cutter works well with the Drunkard Path templates used in this book. A 28 mm cutter is also good to have, especially if you are using a template set that has an inside curve for creating the frame piece.

Olfa 45 mm and 28 mm rotary cutters

Pins

For most of my piecing, I like to use pins with fine, thin shafts that won't distort the fabric. I prefer 0.4 mm Clover Patchwork Pins when I need a shorter pin and thin Clover Flower Head Pins when I need a longer one. Finally, I like to use a specialty pin, the Clover Fork Pin, when I am butting up seams and trying to match corners or points exactly. Although not critical to success, these tools are extremely helpful.

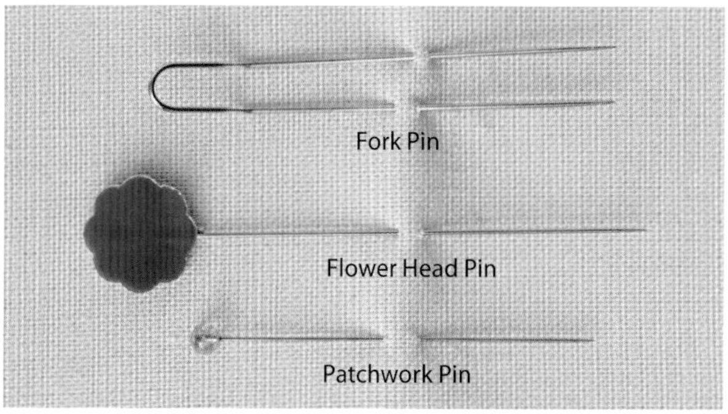

Stylus and Seam Rippers

When sewing curves, you will need to adjust and align the fabric so that the top and bottom layers line up. Alex Anderson's 4-in-1 Essential Sewing Tool provides you with two options: Stiletto or Seam Ripper. Try both options and find out which one works best for you. This tool is nice because it has a long handle and is easy to grasp and maneuver. Another option is a basic seam ripper. I am partial to Bohin's because it has a sharp point and a protective cover that is attached to the seam ripper. Anyone who sews should have a seam ripper on hand because, yes, even the best of us make mistakes.

Alex Anderson's 4-in-1 Essential Sewing Tool; Bohin seam ripper

Seam Guide

Many of the blocks in this book involve sewing across the diagonal of a square.

One approach is to draw a line on the back of the block and sew right on the line. But drawing all those lines can take a lot of time! Using a seam guide eliminates the drawing, and some machines have guides built into their table extensions.

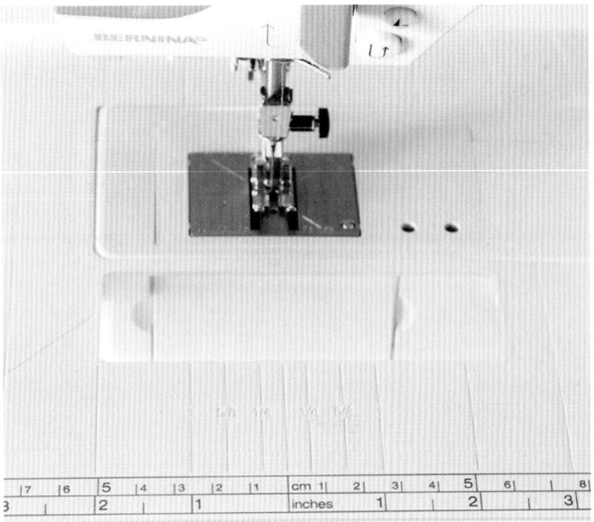

Another option is the Ultimate Seam Guide from C&T Publishing. By aligning the corners of your block with the sewing line on the guide, you can sew without having to mark diagonal lines.

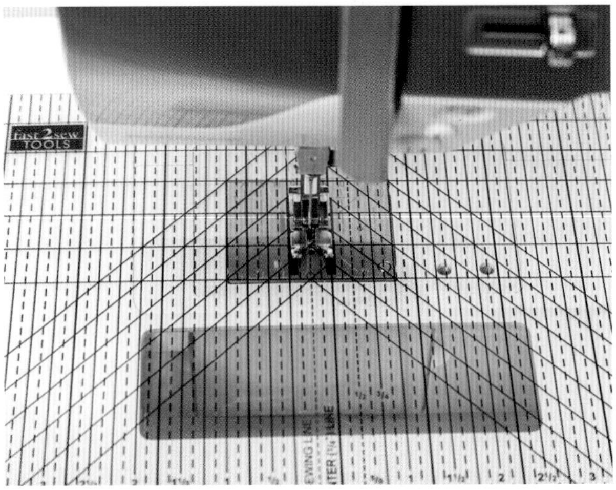

Place the seam guide tool on the bed of your sewing machine and use the markings to sew perfectly across the diagonal of your block.

Design Wall

A design wall can help to improve your design decisions and also organize your quilt top for sewing to minimize mistakes. It can be permanently or temporarily installed.

Using a design wall allows you to step away and look at your quilt from a distance as you try out the placement of fabrics. You might discover that you need to move fabrics around or add a little something as you work to make all the fabrics play nicely together.

A design wall is also a great organizational tool. It can be very easy to get things flipped around when assembling a quilt top—only to sew together a row or set of blocks incorrectly. Using a design wall helps to prevent that. When using a design wall to arrange the pieces for a block, it is useful to have a small cutting mat or square cutting ruler that is at least 12″ × 12″. After you have arranged the fabrics on your design wall, transfer them to your sewing area by placing them on the mat (or ruler).

Search the Internet for different ways of installing a permanent or temporary design wall. It is well worth the time and effort.

working WITH TEMPLATES

A rotary cutter is great for cutting out strips and squares. But when you have peculiar shapes, you need templates. There are just two templates needed to make a Drunkard's Path block and all the quilts in this book.

You can buy commercially made templates or make your own.

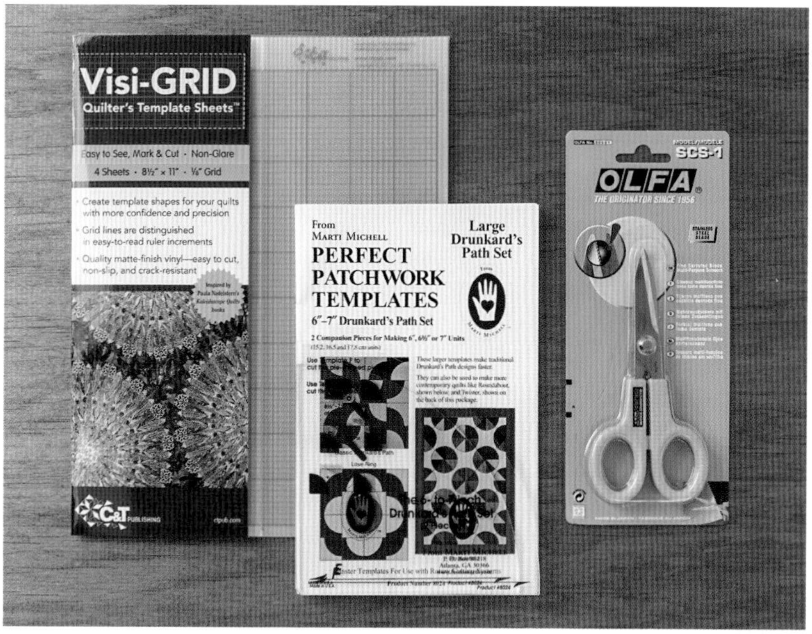

C&T Visi-Grid template plastic; Marti Michell Template Set

Store-Bought Templates

My preferred method is to use commercial templates. Homemade templates might be a good choice for a small project, but cutting out a large number of blocks for a quilt can become overwhelming, and you will find that commercial templates save time and improve accuracy.

For the quilts in this book I used Marti Michell's Large Drunkard's Path Set, but other templates are on the market that you can use. The quilt patterns in this book are based on a 6″ finished block.

Homemade Templates

Making your own templates is economical, and you can make them any size you wish.

When making my own templates, I prefer a template plastic that is marked with a quarter-inch graph. The Visi-Grid Quilter's Template Sheets (by C&T Publishing) are perfect; they are a little thicker than many other template plastics, and the grid marks make it easier to create more accurate templates. If you do use a rotary cutter with one of these templates, you need to be careful that you don't shave off a little of the edge. If you do, your template will not be accurate and your blocks will be wonky.

See Templates (page 78) for patterns to trace.

Making Templates 101

To make templates for all the quilts in this book, use Patterns 1 and 2 (page 78).

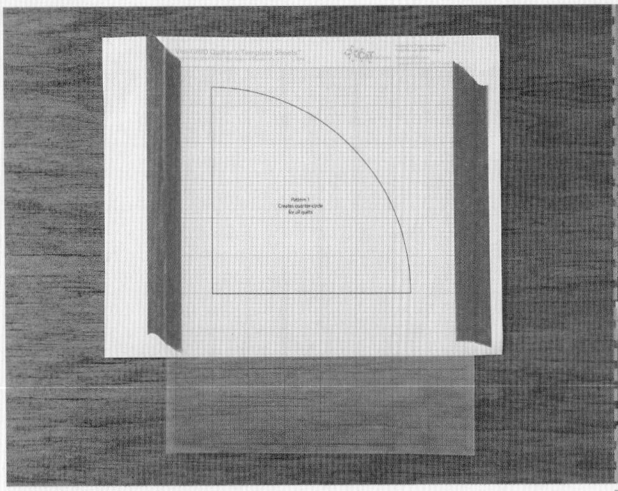

1. Photocopy the template patterns. Check that the shapes were not distorted after copying by verifying that the 1″ square box (provided for scale) actually measures 1″ square. Place the photocopy under the template plastic, aligning the straight lines of the template with the grid marks on the plastic, and tape it in place so it won't slip.

2. With a ruler, trace the straight lines onto the plastic using the lines on the grid as a guide.

3. Make dots or small dashes along curves. You will be able to get a smoother curve by "connecting the dots" when you cut than you would if you tried to cut along a traced line.

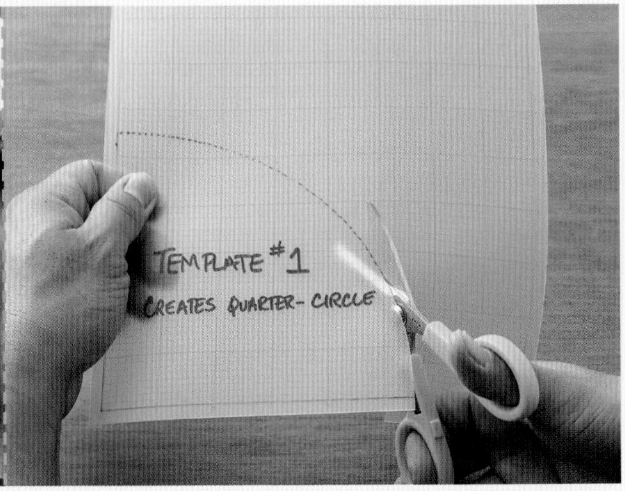

4. Label the template and cut it out with scissors.

sewing

DRUNKARD'S PATH BLOCKS

Curved Piecing

Quilters generally quake in fear over curved piecing. I did too when I first started out. But armed with the right tools, methods, and tips, you will be on your way to sewing curves with confidence.

The first step is to use the features of your sewing machine to your benefit. So grab your manual and see what your machine can do!

TIP: Lost Your Manual?

If you can't find the hard copy of your sewing machine manual, check the manufacturer's website. Many companies have PDF versions you can download.

Needle Down

When sewing curves, you need to stop frequently to adjust the fabric. When you stop sewing, you will want your needle to stop in the down position so that your fabric pieces don't shift. Many machines have a needle-down feature that ensures the needle is in the fabric every time you stop pushing the pedal. Check to see if your machine has this feature, and if it does, make sure it is engaged when sewing curves.

If your machine does not have this option, don't fret. You can manually lower the needle whenever you stop sewing. Just turn the handwheel in a counterclockwise position to lower the needle into the fabric before raising the presser foot.

Presser Foot Up

Just as the needle must be *down* when stopping to adjust the fabric to sew a smooth curve, the presser foot must be *up* so that you can slightly shift the fabric every few stitches. This can be accomplished in many ways. Some machines have a special setting so that the presser foot rises whenever you stop sewing. Other machines have a button to push for raising and lowering the presser foot. Another option is to use a knee lift. This is a bar that fits into your machine and allows you to raise and lower the presser foot with your right knee. Don't have any of these features? Use the lever behind your presser foot.

Drunkard's Path Tutorial

All the patterns in this book include the Drunkard's Path block. Here's my method for creating one.

TIP: Practice! Practice! Practice!

Cut out a few Drunkard's Path blocks from scrap fabric and practice sewing the block. You won't be as concerned if you mess up the scrap block as you would be if you were sewing the "real thing." Sew a practice block when you start up again—you will hone your skills and maybe end up with few blocks that you can turn into a small table runner or pillow.

TIP: Pin Precisely

If your pinning is slightly off, your edges will not align properly when sewn. Small problems add up as you go along.

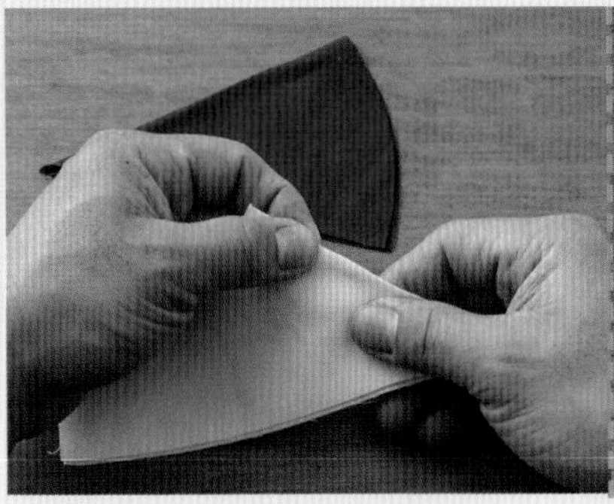

1. Fold each unit in half to find the center point and finger-press.

2. Place the frame unit on top, align the center points, and pin.

3. Align the left edge and pin parallel to the edge of the fabric, with the pinhead sticking out to the right.

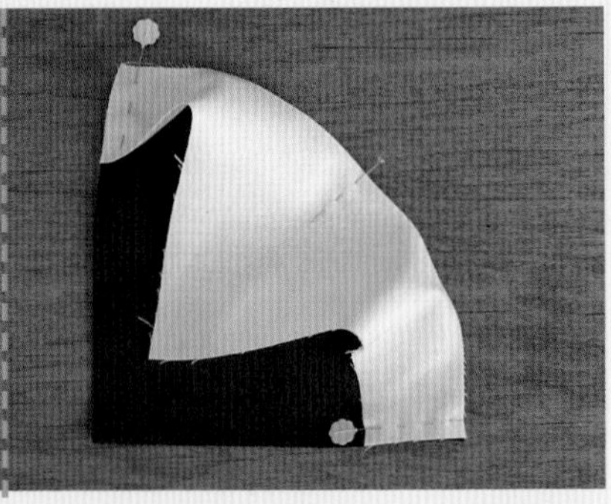

4. Align the other end of the fabric and pin parallel to the edge. The head of the pin should face in to the left.

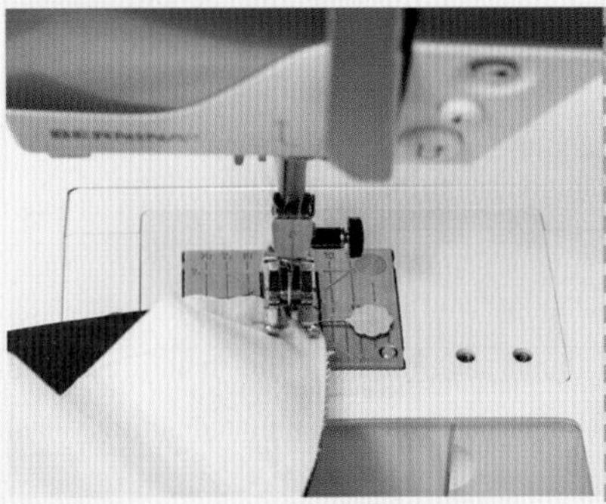

5. Place the block under the presser foot of your sewing machine, lower the foot, and take a few stitches. Remove the pin.

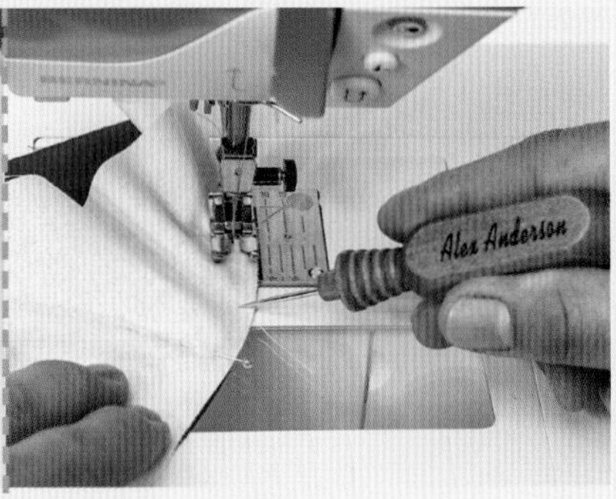

6. Align the edges using a stylus and sew toward the center pin, stopping to adjust the fabric as you go.

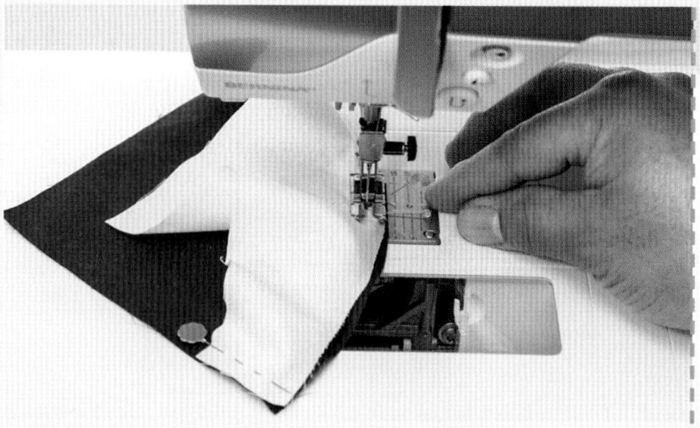

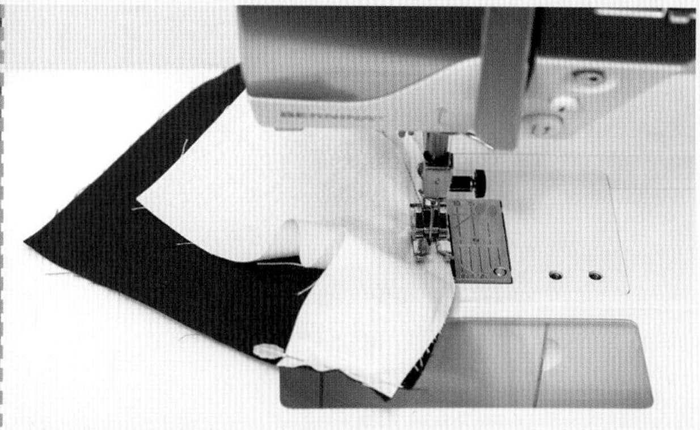

7. Before reaching the center pin, stop sewing. Remove the pin with the needle in the down position.

8. Continue sewing the second half of the curve. You will most likely need to stop frequently to readjust the fabric. Always stop with the needle in the down position and raise the presser foot to manipulate the fabric so that it flattens out.

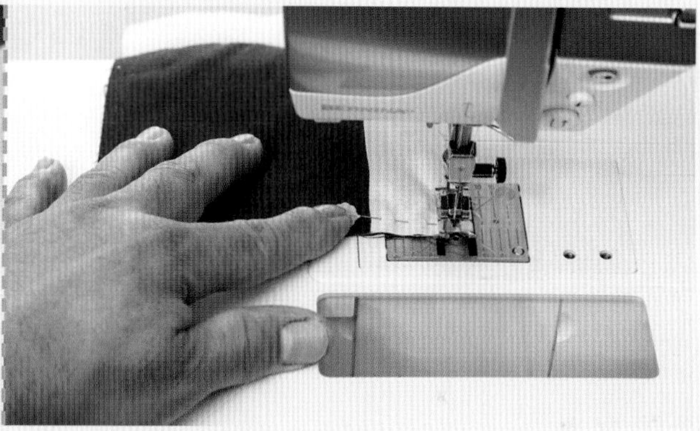

9. When the fabric is smoothed out, you are ready to finish the seam.

10. Sew to the edge of the block. Use the head of the pin to guide and adjust the fabric as you sew to the edge.

11. Pick up another block and chain piece it together.

TIP: Chain Piecing

Chain piecing is a great way to sew efficiently. Once you have sewn a block, pick up another one and sew the seam without clipping the thread. Continue in an assembly-line fashion until you have a long strand of sewn blocks. Remove the strand from the machine and cut the thread between the individual blocks.

Finished Drunkard's Path block;
press the seam as directed in the pattern.

Block Variations

The projects in this book often involve altering the Drunkard's Path block. Detailed instructions for each variation are here.

Corner Triangle Variation

This variation is used in Bowties *(page 22)*, Tile Floor *(page 39)*, Nightfall *(page 44)*, *and* Shaken Not Stirred *(page 58)*.

A half-square triangle is sewn to one or both corners of the block. The patterns in this book use a square that measures 2½″ × 2½″.

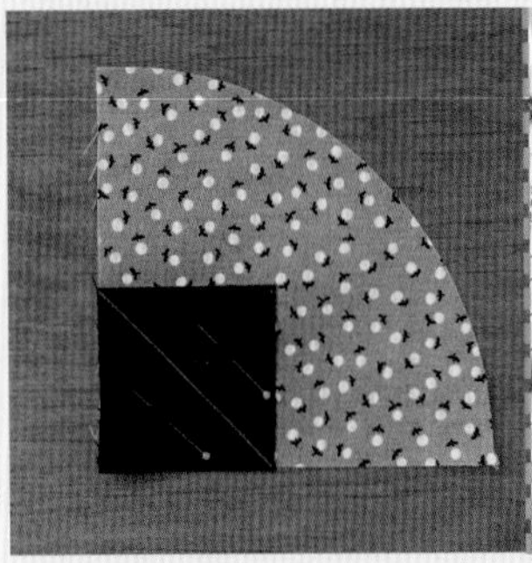

1. Draw a diagonal line on the wrong side of the fabric and place the square on the corner of the quarter-circle unit. Pin if necessary.

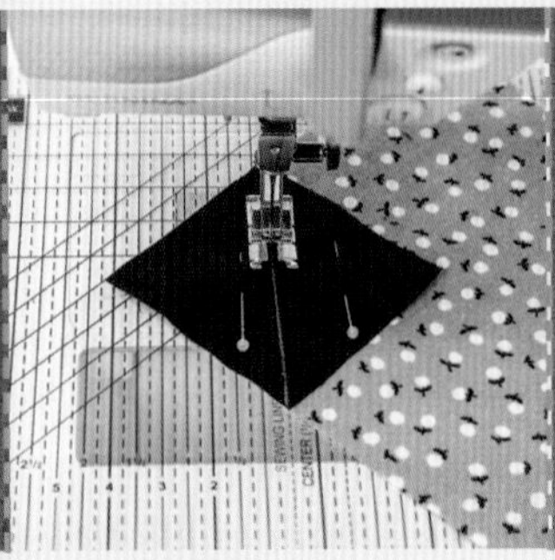

2. Sew directly on the drawn line.

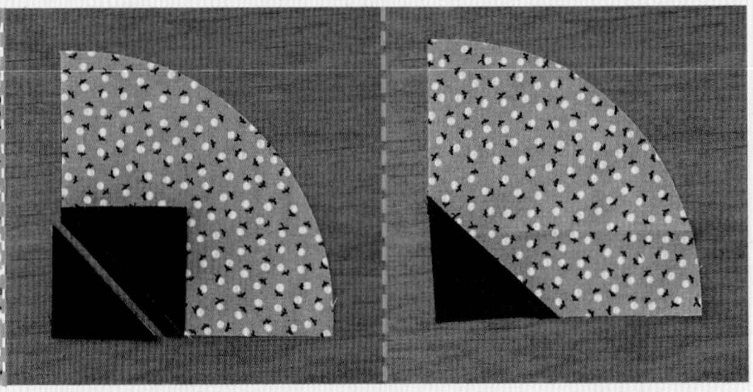

3. Trim away the excess, leaving a ¼″ seam allowance, and press seams according to pattern directions.

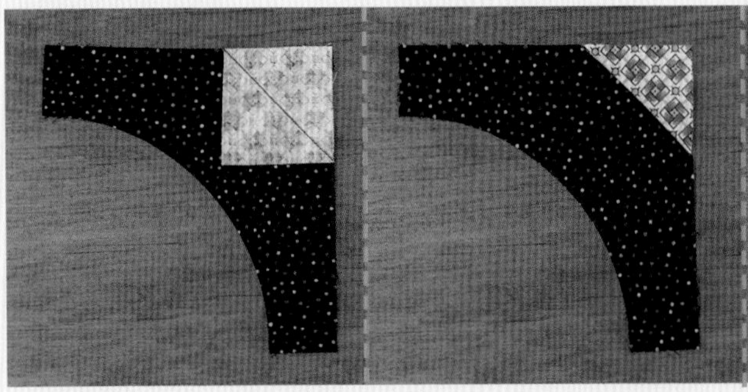

4. Repeat the same process to create the corner triangle on the frame unit.

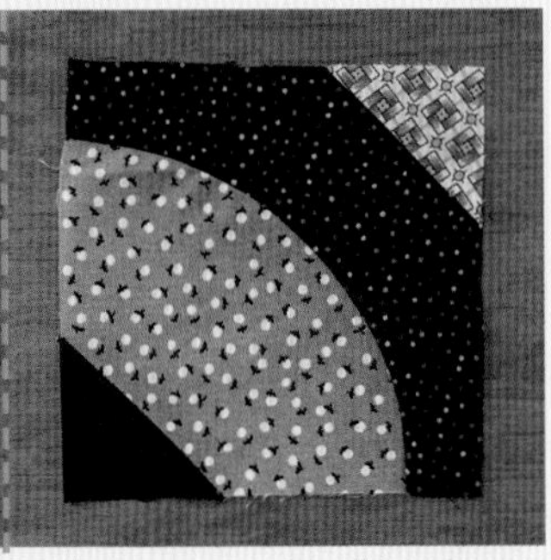

5. Sew together the quarter-circle and frame units following the directions in the Drunkard's Path Tutorial (page 12).

Fan Variation

This variation is used in Abstract *(page 49).*

The fan variation is made by first creating half-square triangle blocks and then using the templates to trim these into the proper shapes. The half-square triangle units finish slightly larger than needed, allowing you the opportunity to square-up.

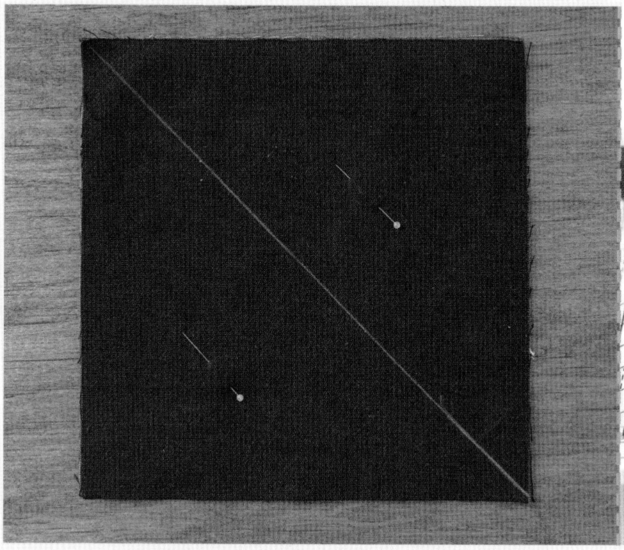

1. Draw a diagonal line on the wrong side of one of the fabrics. Place 2 pieces right sides together.

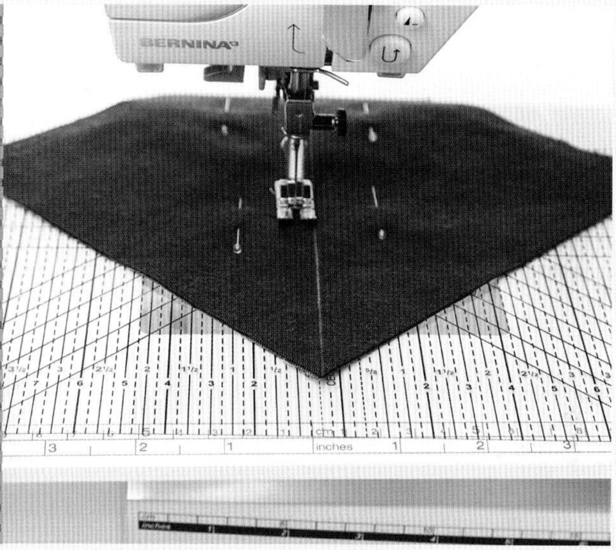

2. Align your quarter-inch foot to rest on the line and sew a ¼″ seam to the left of the drawn line.

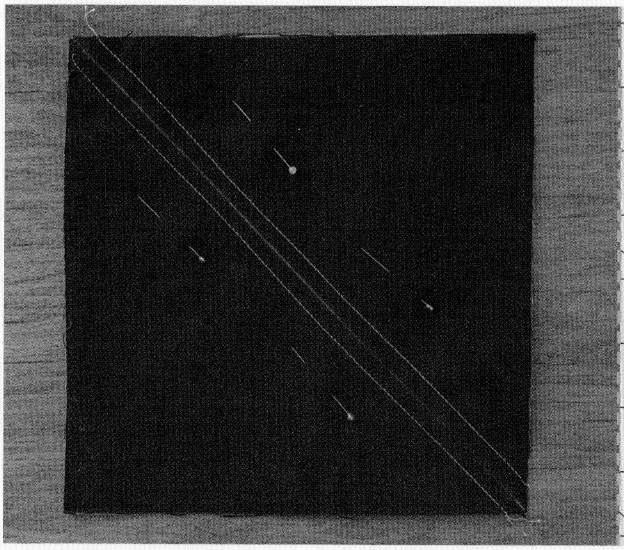

3. Repeat this process and sew a second line of stitching on the other side of the line.

4. Cut the block apart directly on the line and press according to the pattern directions.

5. Trim the block to proper size as listed in the pattern.

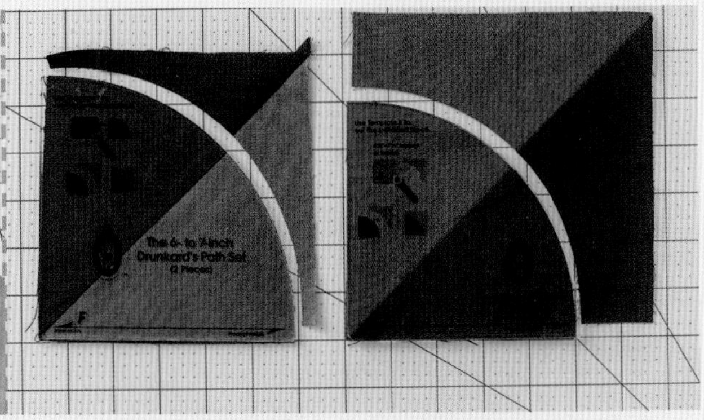

6. Use the individual templates to cut out the quarter-circle and frame units. Be careful about which way the fabric is aligned so that you have the correct light-dark orientation.

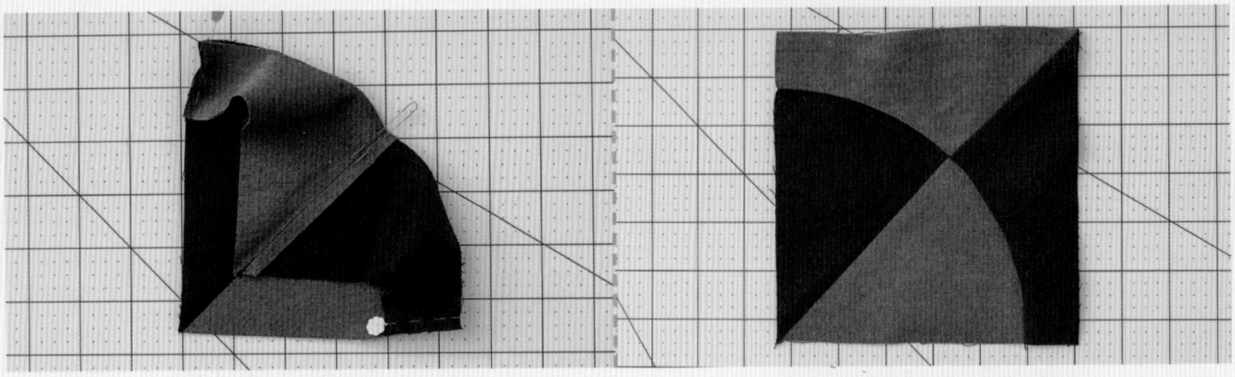

7. Pin the block using Clover Flower Head Pins and Fork Pins. Sew together the quarter-circle and frame units following the Drunkard's Path Tutorial (page 12).

Fan and Triangle Variation

This variation is used in Millstones *(page 62).*

This variation builds on the previous two. A half-square triangle is added to the corners to make this block. Follow the directions for the Corner Triangle Variation (page 14).

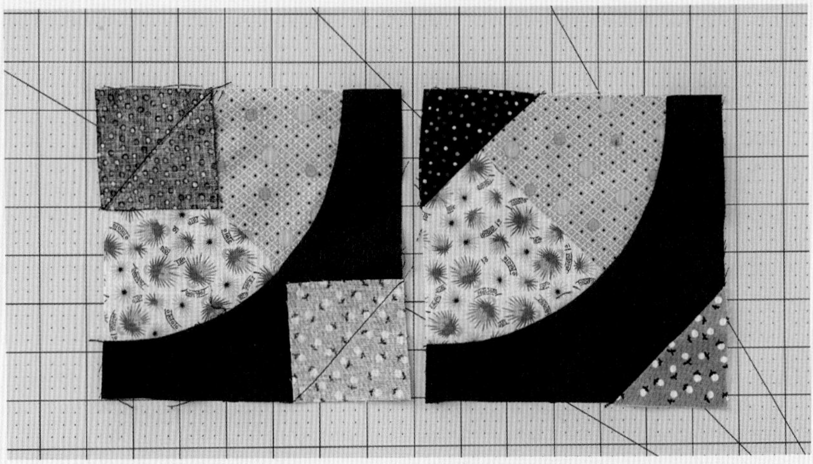

Fan and Half-Square Triangle Variation

This variation is used in Test Pattern *(page 34).*

1. Begin with half-square triangle units that measure 2½″ × 2½″ (including seam allowances). If you are starting from scratch, begin with 2 squares of fabric that measure 3″ × 3″ and follow the directions for creating half-square triangle blocks as explained in Fan Variation (page 15). Trim the resulting units to 2½″ × 2½″.

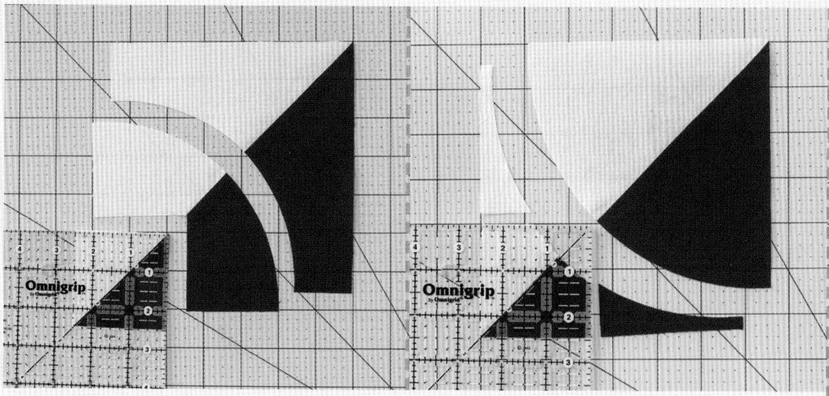

2. Triangle units can also be created by using the waste material from both the frame and quarter-circle units. Align your ruler on the corner and trim so you have a square 2½″ × 2½″. Note that units made from the waste of the quarter-circle unit will have a little piece missing. Not to worry—that part of the block will be cut off anyway when the unit is added to the block.

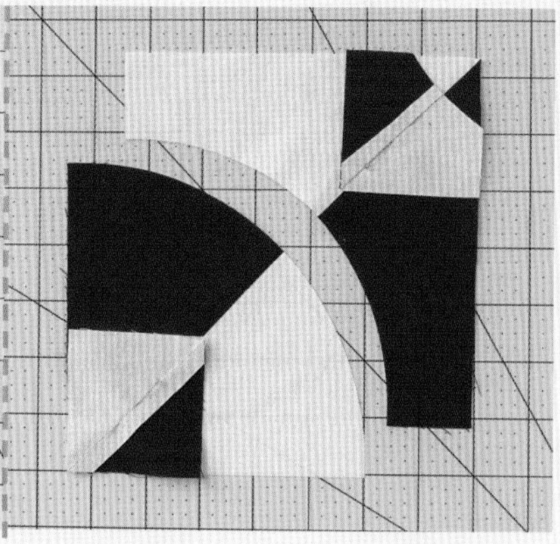

3. Draw a diagonal line on the wrong side of the half-square triangle units. Position and pin these units on the quarter-circle and frame units, making certain the values alternate. For units that have the missing sections, place that portion of the block toward the corner.

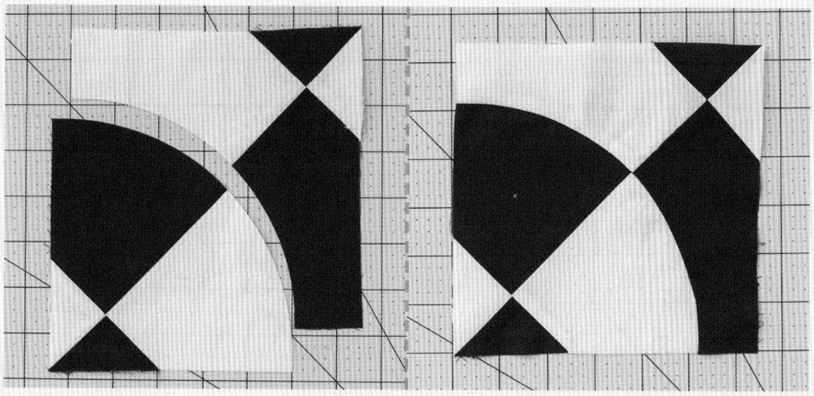

4. Stitch on the line, trim away the excess, and press the seams.

5. Sew together the quarter-circle and frame units following the directions for curved piecing in the Drunkard's Path Tutorial (page 12).

Sixteen-Patch Variation

This variation is used in Abstract *(page 49) and* Checkerboard *(page 65).*

1. Make a Sixteen-Patch block (4 across and 4 down) that finishes 5½″ × 5½″ (including seam allowances) using your preferred method. Each square of the sixteen-patch should be cut 1¾″ × 1¾″.

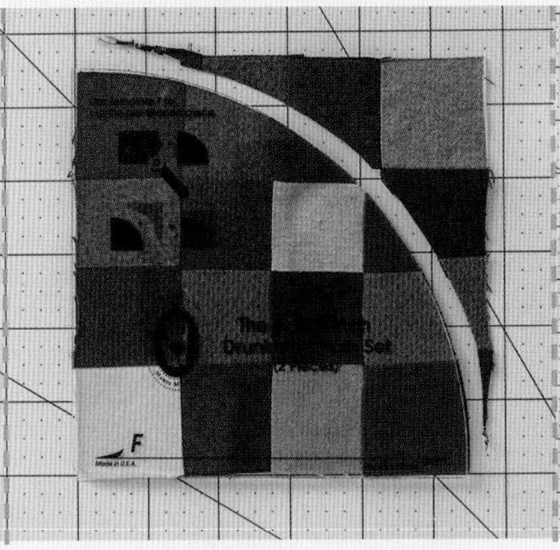

2. Subcut the Sixteen-Patch block into quarter-circles using Template 1. Depending on the pattern, you might need to be conscious of the color of the corner square.

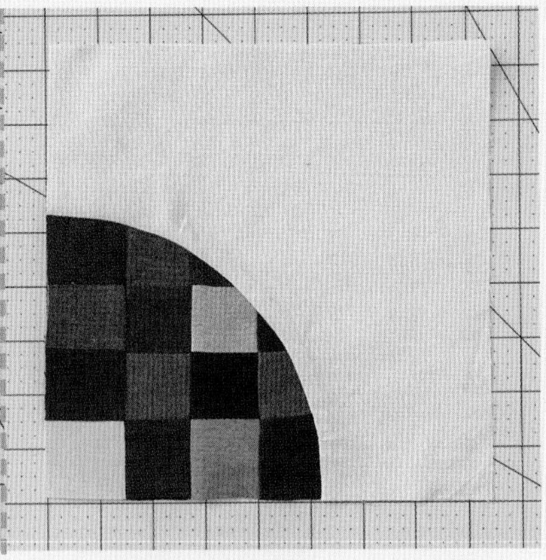

3. Sew this unit to a frame unit following the instructions for curved piecing in the Drunkard's Path Tutorial (page 12).

Rail Fence Variation

This variation is used in Beach Balls *(page 26),* Snake in the Grass *(page 54), and* Peacock Alley *(page 70).*

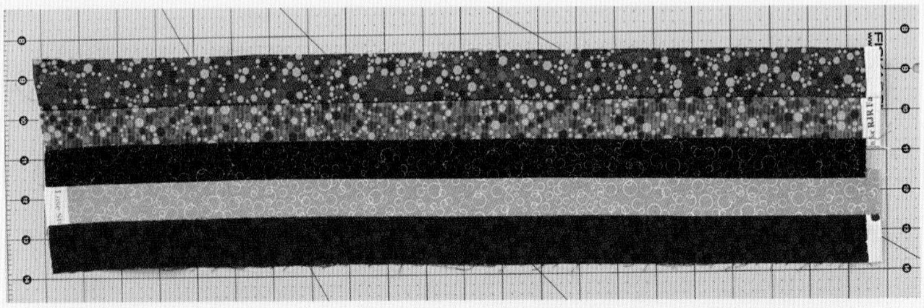

1. Create a strip set using your preferred method. For the template in this book, the strip-set unit should measure 5½″ tall (including seam allowances). Each strip should be cut 1¾″ wide.

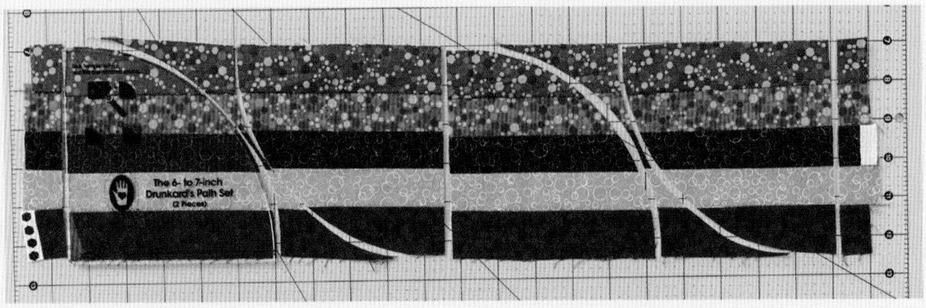

2. Subcut the strip set into quarter-circles using Template 1.

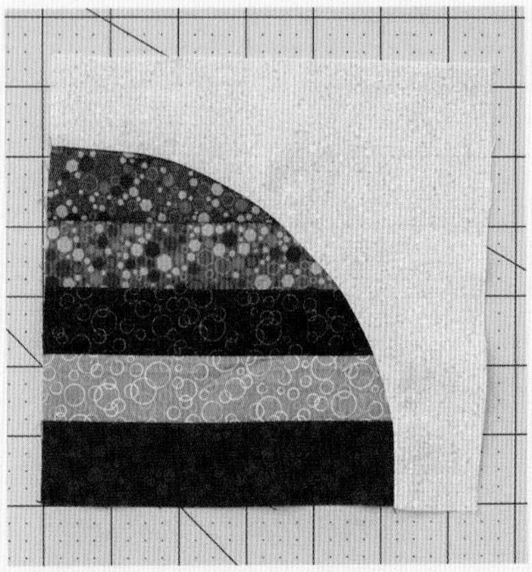

3. Sew together the quarter-circle and frame units following the directions for curved piecing in the Drunkard's Path Tutorial (page 12).

Border Options

Putting a little time and thought into the border can add a lot to a quilt. Consider using the Drunkard's Path block and some of its variations the next time you are looking for a border treatment with pizzazz.

Corner Triangle Variation

Add interest by framing a quilt using the Corner Triangle Variation (page 14).

Detail of *Peacock Alley* center border

Detail of *Shaken Not Stirred* outer border

Rail Fence Variation

The Rail Fence Variation (previous page) is very versatile. Change the width of the pieces of the strip set or vary the number of strips.

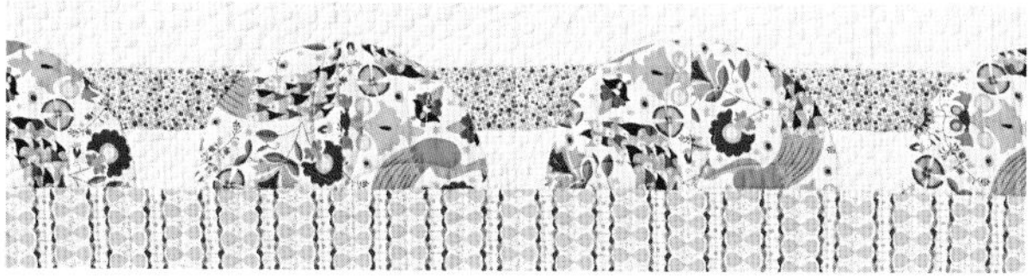

Detail of *Peacock Alley* outer border

Experiment with some of the other block variations to see what creative border treatments you can invent.

Detail of *Checkerboard* outer border

quiltmaking IN A BUSY WORLD

Some of the quilts in this book have a lot of "parts," and making the whole quilt can seem like a daunting task. Maybe you fear that you just don't have enough time. Break down the job into manageable steps, and you can get it done bit-by-bit, with your sanity intact.

Too often we think we need an entire day to work on a project, but those days can be few and far between. Identifying small steps that can be done in 15- or 30-minute segments may fit better with how you actually live. Some tasks can be done while you are doing something else—watching TV, talking on the phone, or having your morning coffee. Carve out small amounts of time during the day and chip away at the bits and pieces of a quilt. Before you know it, the project will be done.

Here are some tips on how to turn big quilts into a series of small (and joyful) tasks.

Manageable Bites

- Cut out the fabric as listed in the supply list. That's *it*—take the time to *just* cut the fabric. Group together fabrics for a particular block or quilt section.
- Work on part of a block. Mark the backs of squares destined to become half-square triangles and plan to sew them later. Or sew together some strip sets.
- Pin the Drunkard's Path units together or pin together other block components. When you are finished prepping that part of the pattern, toss those pieces by the sewing machine and they will be ready for you to sew when you have time.
- Sew together prepped units. If they are already prepped, it will be an easy job to just sit down and sew a few (or all) of them together. If you know how the seams need to be pressed and have the time, go ahead with that step too.
- Put blocks on a design wall and play around with their arrangement. When you are happy, begin to sew the quilt together in sections. You don't have to do it all in one sitting! It will be easy to sew together a few blocks, or part of a row, if it's all there in front of you. Take down a few blocks, sew them together, and put them back up. You can walk away, and later, when you have time, come back and pick up where you left off.
- Even when you have more time, taking a break may be a good idea. Seeing double? Making a lot of errors? Get up from the machine, turn it off, walk away, and do something else! Return later that day, or the next, to pick up where you left off. Sometimes it is better to let the dust settle and resume when you are in a better frame of mind.

PROJECTS

BOWTIES

Finished block: 6˝ × 6˝ • **Finished quilt:** 86˝ × 92˝

This quilt gains its sparkle from the scrappiness of the fabric choices. I used 1930s reproductions and let them sing with black backgrounds. If this is a bit on the dark side for you, pick a light background and then add your favorite colors. You can switch it up a bit more by replacing some or all of the quarter-circle units with the Fan and Triangle Variation (page 16).

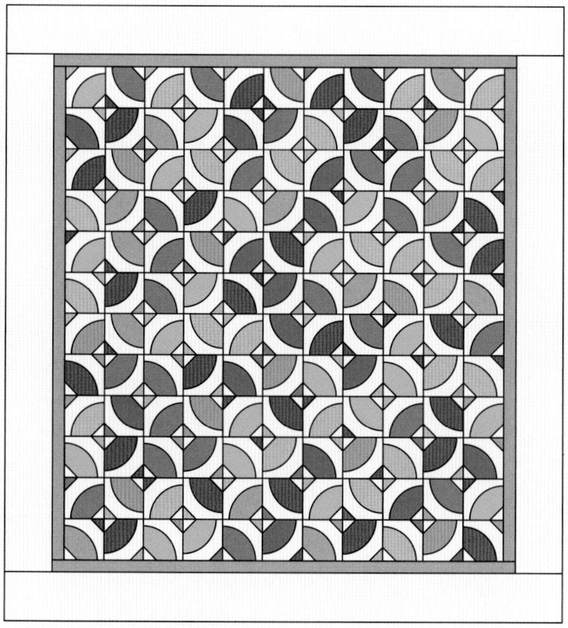

Changing the black background and red border to lighter colors gives the quilt a new look.

Selected blocks are replaced with the Fan and Triangle Variation (page 16).

Materials

I used reproduction 1930s designs for the prints and a mix of solids and subtle prints for the tonal blacks.

Prints: 11 assorted fabrics, ½ yard of each

Tonal blacks: 11 assorted fabrics, ⅝ yard of each

Red: ¾ yard

Black: 2¾ yards

Backing: 8 yards

Batting: 94″ × 100″

Binding: 1⅛ yards red (½″ finished width)

Cutting

To make templates for cutting quarter-circles and frames, use Patterns 1 and 2 (page 78).

Prints

- Cut 2 strips 5½″ × width of fabric from each of the selections.

  Subcut 12 quarter-circle units from each fabric using Template 1. You will have 132 pieces.

- Cut 12 squares 2½″ × 2½″ from each fabric. You will have 132 squares.

Tonal blacks

- Cut 2 strips 6½″ × width of fabric from each fabric.

  Subcut 12 squares 6½″ × 6½″ from each fabric.

  Subcut into frames using Template 2. You will have 132 pieces.

  From the quarter-circle waste fabric:

  Cut 132 squares 2½″ × 2½″.

Red

- Cut 8 strips 2½″ × width of fabric.

Black

- Cut 2 strips parallel to the selvage 8½″ × 76½″.
- Cut 2 strips parallel to the selvage 8½″ × 86½″.

TIP

If your solid black fabric is wide enough and you cut carefully, you might be able to cut some squares 6½″ × 6½″ to use together with your black tonal selections.

Backing

- Cut 3 pieces 94″ × width of fabric.

Binding

- Cut 10 strips 3½″ × width of fabric. (This is for a ½″ finished binding. If you prefer a narrower binding, cut accordingly.)

Construction

Seam allowances are ¼″. For detailed instructions on how to create this block, refer to Corner Triangle Variation (page 14).

Block Assembly

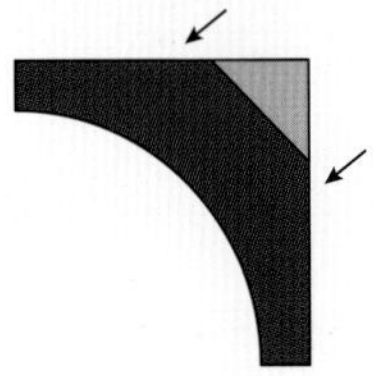

Make 132.

1. Sew the print squares 2½″ × 2½″ onto the black frame pieces to make half-square triangles. Trim away the excess fabric, leaving a ¼″ seam allowance. Press the seams toward the black.

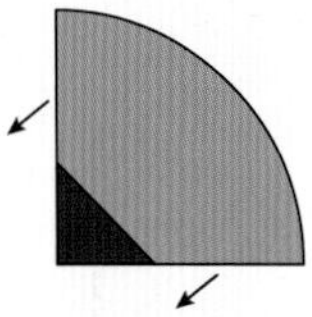

Make 132.

2. Sew a tonal black square 2½″ × 2½″ onto a quarter-circle block to make a half-square triangle corner. Trim away the excess fabric, leaving a ¼″ seam allowance. Press the seam toward the black.

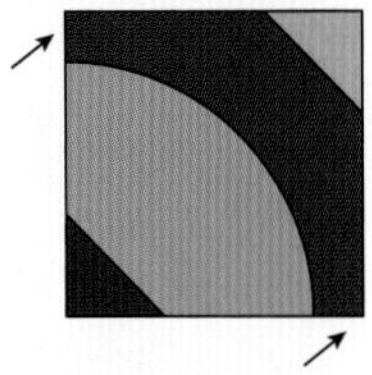

Make 132.

3. Sew together the quarter-circle and frame units to form the block. Press the seams toward the black.

Quilt Construction

Bowties assembly

1. Randomly arrange the blocks following the *Bowties* assembly diagram. Reposition the blocks until you are pleased with the fabric placement.

2. Sew the blocks together into rows. Press the seams in opposite directions from row to row so that the seams nest.

3. Sew the rows together. Press the seams as you wish.

Borders

1. Trim the selvages off the 2½″-wide red strips and stitch them together end to end on the diagonal. Subcut into 2 strips 2½″ × 72½″ and 2 strips 2½″ × 70½″.

2. Sew the 2 red border strips 2½″ × 72½″ onto the sides of the quilt. Press the seams toward the red border.

3. Sew the 2 red border strips 2½″ × 70½″ to the top and bottom of the quilt. Press the seams toward the red border.

4. Sew the 2 black border pieces 8½″ × 76½″ onto the sides of the quilt. Press the seams toward the red border.

5. Sew the 2 black border pieces 8½″ × 86½″ to the top and bottom of the quilt. Press the seams toward the red border.

Finishing

1. Trim the selvage edges of the 3 backing pieces and join them together along the 94″ sides.

2. Layer, baste, and quilt as desired.

3. Sew together the 3½″-wide binding strips on the diagonal.

4. Attach the binding to the quilt with a ½″ seam allowance using your preferred method.

BEACH BALLS

Finished block: 6˝ × 6˝ • **Finished quilt:** 66˝ × 84˝

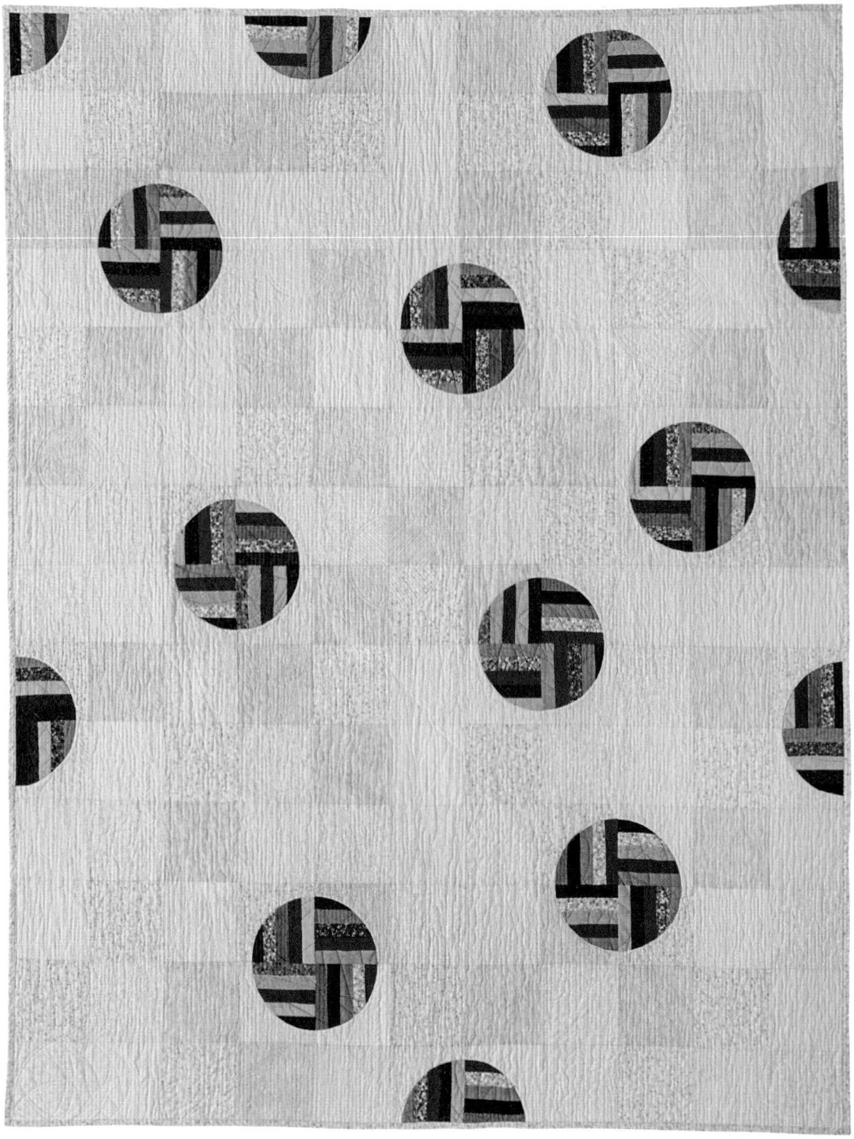

Brights contrast starkly against a light, neutral background to create beach balls that make this quilt a vision of summer fun. I used fabrics from Patrick Lose's ***Basically Patrick*** *line for RJR Fabrics to create the floating balls and a range of tans to suggest sand. If you want a scrappier look or more color variety—go for it. Simply adjust the number of strips that you cut from each fabric and make sure you have variety in color and value. For the background, choose a group of fabrics of similar value that showcase the strip-set fabrics. You can even take a ride on the dark side with a black background that makes the ball colors pop. A smaller version makes a great baby quilt.*

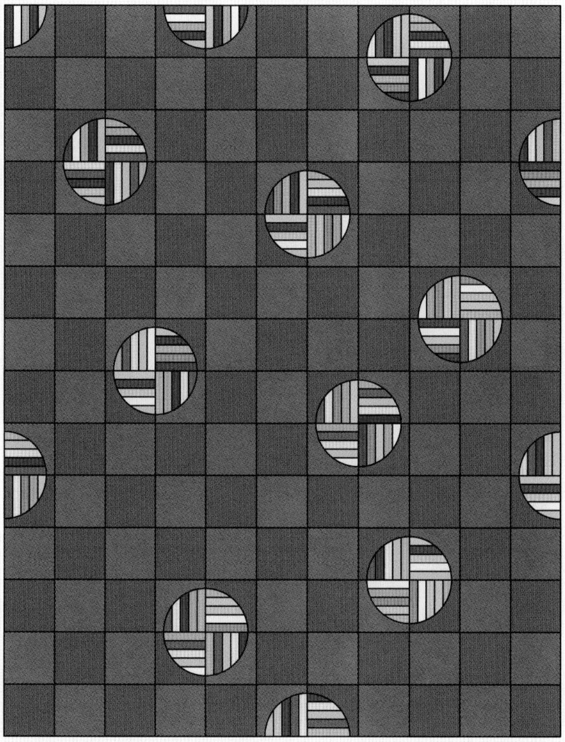

A darker background gives the quilt a different look.

A smaller version makes a great baby quilt.

DESIGN IDEA

Experiment with the placement of the balls when you arrange your blocks. Or use some of the other block variations presented in this book in place of the strip sets.

Materials

3 light colors: ¼ yard or 1 fat quarter of each

4 medium colors: ¼ yard or 1 fat quarter of each

4 dark colors: ¼ yard or 1 fat quarter of each

6 light creams and 6 light tans: ¾ yard of each

Backing: 5¼ yards

Batting: 74″ × 92″

Binding: 1 yard light cream or tan (½″ finished width)

Cutting

To make templates for cutting, use Patterns 1 and 2 (page 78).

Light, medium, and dark colors

You can use ¼-yard cuts, fat quarters, or a mix. When done cutting, you will have 66 strips 1½″ × approximately 20″.

From yardage:

- Cut 3 strips 1½″ × width of fabric from each fabric.

  Cut each strip in half widthwise.

From fat quarters:

- Cut 6 strips 1½″ × 20″ from each.

Light creams and tans

- Cut 3 strips 6½″ × width of fabric from each fabric.

  Subcut into 13 squares 6½″ × 6½″ from each fabric. You will have 156. You need 154 for the quilt.

Backing

- Cut 2 pieces 92″ × width of fabric.

Binding

- Cut 9 strips of cream or tan 3½″ × width of fabric. (This is for a ½″ finished binding. If you prefer a narrower binding, cut accordingly.)

Construction

Seam allowances are ¼″. For detailed instructions on how to create this block, refer to Rail Fence Variation (page 18).

Make Strip Sets with Colored Fabrics

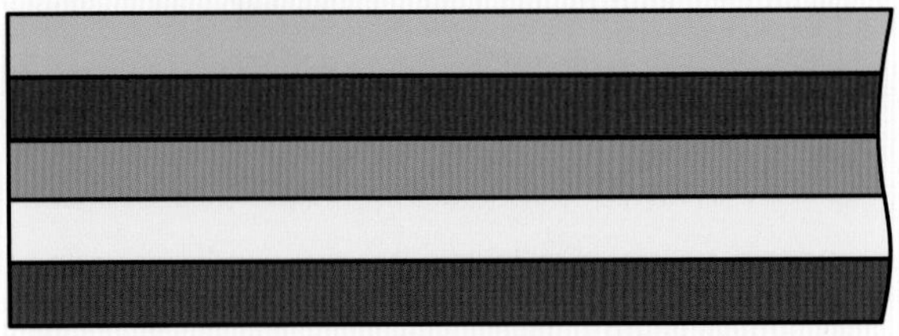

Make 13.

1. Sew together 5 colored strips 1½″ × approximately 20″ in random order, alternating the light, medium, and dark colors. Press the seams in each strip set in one direction. You will have 1 extra strip.

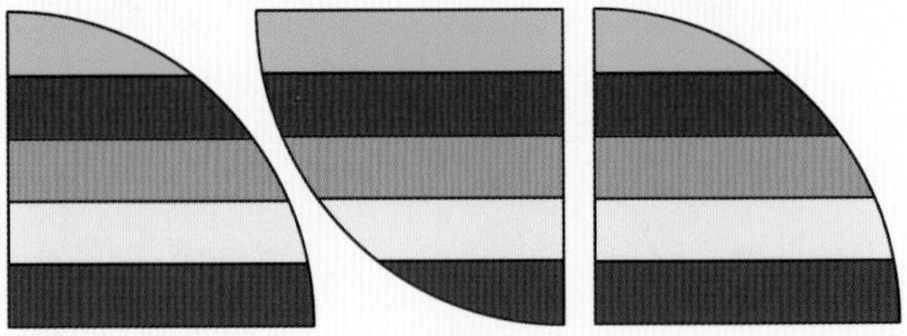

2. Cut 4 quarter-circles from each strip set using Template 1. You will need only 43 for the quilt. The 9 extra units will allow you some design flexibility.

DESIGN IDEA

Have extra quarter-circle units? Make a pillow by cutting four more frame units and sewing four blocks. Sew together the blocks to make a 12″ pillow. For a slightly larger pillow, add borders or cut the frame pieces slightly larger as in Millstones *(page 62). For a great table runner, join several blocks.*

Block Construction

1. Arrange the light cream and light tan squares 6½″ × 6½″ as shown in the *Beach Balls* assembly diagram. Randomly mix the creams and tans as you arrange the blocks 11 across and 14 down.

2. Place the quarter-circle units on top of some cream and tan squares, using the quilt assembly diagram for reference. Rearrange the units until you are pleased with their placement.

3. Remove a tan square and its corresponding quarter-circle unit. Create the frames using Template 2. Sew together the 2 units. Press the seams of adjacent quarter-circle units in opposite directions so that they nest. Place the unit back on the design wall in its proper place.

4. Repeat this process for the remainder of the tan and quarter-circle units.

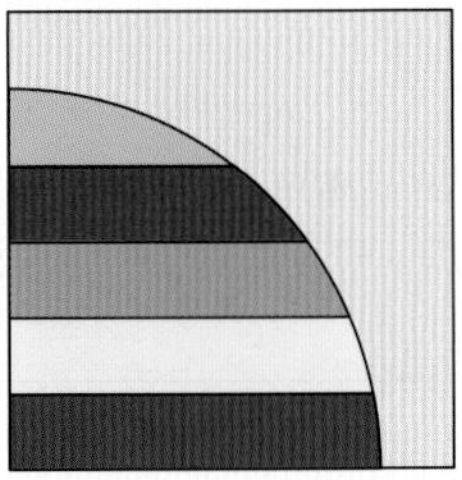

Quilt Construction

Beach Balls assembly

1. Sew the blocks together into rows. Press the seams in opposite directions from row to row so that the seams nest.

2. Sew the rows together. Press the seams as you wish.

Finishing

1. Trim the selvage edges of the 2 backing pieces and join them together along the 92″ sides.

2. Layer, baste, and quilt as desired.

3. Sew together the 3½″-wide binding strips on the diagonal.

4. Attach the binding to the quilt with a ½″ seam allowance using your preferred method.

DECO BLUE

Finished block: 8˝ × 8˝ • **Finished quilt:** 90˝ × 90˝

Deco Blue gets its Art Deco feeling with earthy blues from Michael Miller's **Cotton Couture collection***, but the design lends itself to many palettes. Browns, greens, and muted reds give it a bit of an Arts and Crafts feel. The key is to choose a background color that allows the graphic elements of the quilt to stand out. Play around with your favorite color combinations and see what happens!*

Warm pastels push *Deco Blue* into spring. Florals would be nice for the quarter-circle pieces.

A variety of colors gives a new look to the quilt. This would be a wonderful way to use batiks.

Materials

Dark blue: ⅞ yard

Medium gray-blue: 3⅝ yards

White: 3¼ yards

Light gray: 1 yard

Medium gray: ⅝ yard

Dark gray: ¾ yard

Dark indigo or black: ¾ yard

Backing: 8¼ yards

Batting: 98″ × 98″

Binding: 1⅛ yards dark indigo or black (½″ finished width)

Cutting

To make templates for cutting, use Patterns 1 and 2 (page 78).

Dark blue

- Cut 4 strips 5½″ × width of fabric.

  Subcut into 32 quarter-circles with Template 1.

Medium gray-blue

- Cut 4 strips 5½″ × width of fabric.

  Subcut into 32 quarter-circles with Template 1.

- Cut 2 strips parallel to the selvage 8½″ × 74½″.

- Cut 2 strips parallel to the selvage 8½″ × 90½″.

White

Block A:

- Cut 8 strips 8½″ × width of fabric.

  Subcut into 32 squares 8½″ × 8½″.

  Subcut into frames using Template 2.

Block B:

- Cut 6 strips 6½″ × width of fabric.

  Subcut into 32 squares 6½″ × 6½″.

  Subcut into frames using Template 2.

  From the quarter-circle waste fabric:

  Cut 32 squares 2½″ × 2½″.

Cutting continued on page 32.

Cutting continued.

Light gray

- Cut 2 strips 6½″ × width of fabric.

  Subcut into 32 rectangles 2½″ × 6½″.

- Cut 8 strips 1½″ × width of fabric.

Medium gray

- Cut 2 strips 6½″ × width of fabric.

  Subcut into 32 rectangles 2½″ × 6½″.

Dark gray

- Cut 8 strips 2½″ × width of fabric.

Dark indigo or black

- Cut 8 strips 2½″ × width of fabric.

Backing

- Cut 3 pieces 98″ × width of fabric.

Binding

- Cut 10 strips 3½″ × width of fabric. (This is for a ½″ finished binding. If you prefer a narrower binding, adjust accordingly.)

Construction

Seam allowances are ¼″. For detailed instructions on how to create this block, refer to the Drunkard's Path Tutorial (page 12).

Block Assembly

Block A

Sew together a white frame piece cut from the 8½″ × 8½″ square and a dark blue quarter-circle piece. Press the seam toward the dark blue.

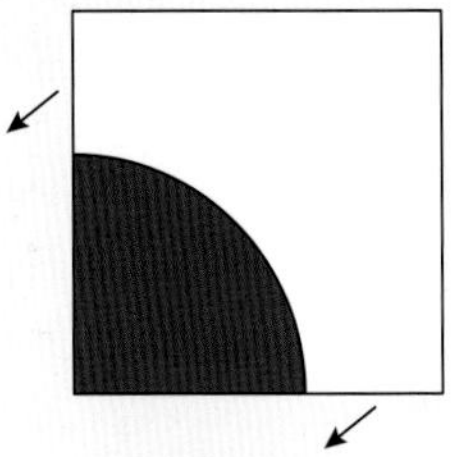

Make 32.

Block B

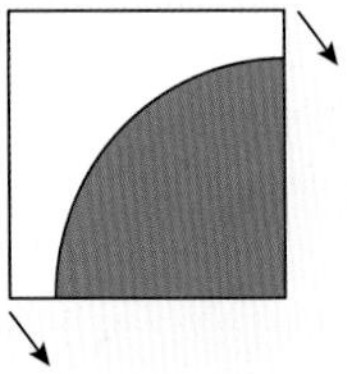

Make 32.

1. Sew together a white frame piece cut from the 6½″ × 6½″ square and a medium gray-blue quarter-circle piece. Press toward the white.

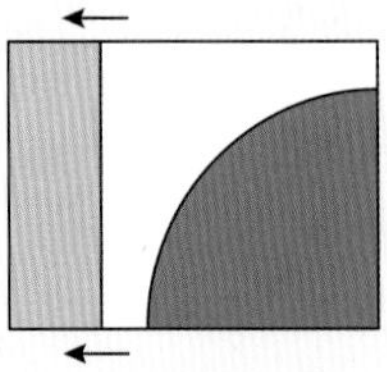

Make 32.

2. Sew a light gray piece 2½″ × 6½″ to each unit. Press toward the light gray.

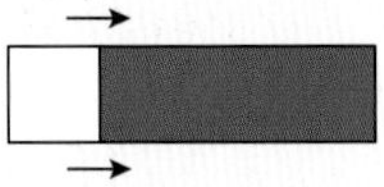

Make 32.

3. Sew a medium gray piece 2½″ × 6½″ to a white 2½″ × 2½″ square. Press toward the medium gray.

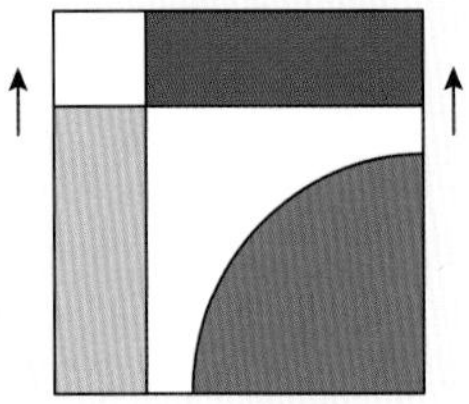

Make 32.

4. Sew the Step 3 unit to the Step 2 block. Press toward the dark gray.

Quilt Construction

Deco Blue assembly

1. Arrange the blocks following the *Deco Blue* assembly diagram.

2. Sew the blocks together into rows. Press the seams in opposite directions from row to row so that the seams nest.

3. Sew the rows together. Press the seams as you wish.

Borders

Dark Gray

1. Trim the selvages from the 8 dark gray strips 2½″ × width of fabric and stitch them together on the diagonal. Subcut into 2 strips 2½″ × 64½″ and 2 strips 2½″ × 68½″.

2. Sew the 2½″ × 64½″ strips to the sides of the quilt. Press the seams toward the dark gray.

3. Sew the 2½″ × 68½″ strips to the top and bottom of the quilt. Press the seams toward the dark gray.

Light Gray

1. Trim the selvages from the 8 light gray strips 1½″ × width of fabric and stitch them together on the diagonal. Subcut into 2 strips 1½″ × 68½″ and 2 strips 1½″ × 70½″.

2. Sew the strips 1½″ × 68½″ to the sides of the quilt. Press the seams toward the dark gray.

3. Sew the strips 1½″ × 70½″ to the top and bottom of the quilt. Press the seams toward the dark gray.

Dark Indigo or Black

1. Trim the selvages from the 8 dark indigo/black strips 2½″ × width of fabric and stitch them together on the diagonal. Subcut into 2 strips 2½″ × 70½″ and 2 strips 2½″ × 74½″.

2. Sew the strips 2½″ × 70½″ to the sides of the quilt. Press the seams toward the dark indigo/black.

3. Sew the strips 2½″ × 74½″ to the top and bottom of the quilt. Press the seams toward the dark indigo/black.

Medium Gray-Blue

1. Sew the 2 medium gray-blue strips 8½″ × 74½″ to the sides of the quilt. Press the seams toward the dark indigo/black.

2. Sew the 2 medium gray-blue strips 8½″ × 90½″ to the top and bottom of the quilt. Press the seams toward the dark indigo/black.

Finishing

1. Trim the selvage edges of the 3 backing pieces and join them together along the 98″ sides.

2. Layer, baste, and quilt as desired.

3. Sew together the 3½″-wide binding strips on the diagonal.

4. Attach the binding to the quilt with a ½″ seam allowance using your preferred method.

TEST PATTERN

Finished blocks: 6˝ × 6˝, 12˝ × 12˝ • **Finished quilt:** 63˝ × 63˝

This red-and-white quilt gets a color punch from the addition of a little yellow. If red and white isn't your style, pick your favorite color and a neutral background, and add a third color to give it a bit of pop! I challenge you to try some colors that you might not normally pick—they may just be the ones that give your quilt a little spice.

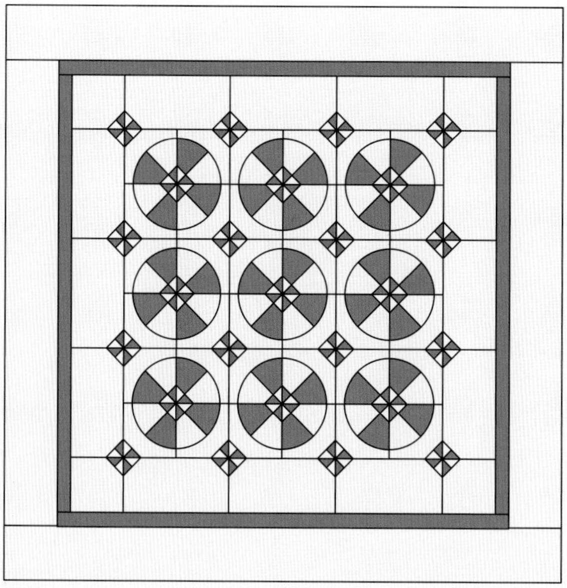

Blues and creams give this quilt a calmer feel. The light yellow adds just the right punch.

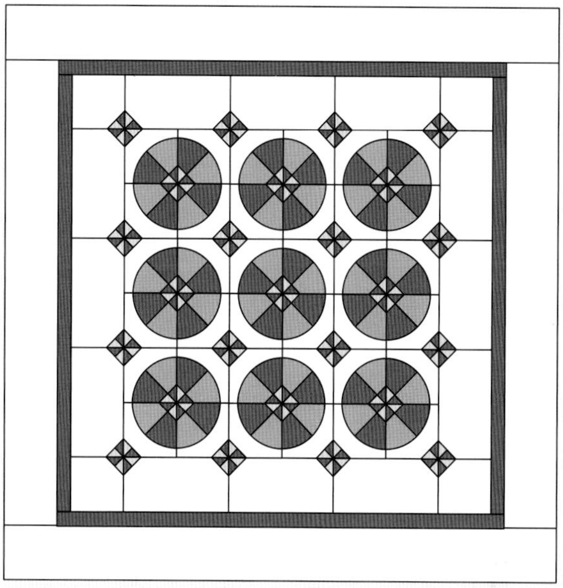

Consider replacing the background color in the fans with a color to complement the other fan blade. Circles emerge and give the quilt a totally different look.

Materials

White: 4 yards

Yellow: ½ yard

Red: 1⅜ yards

Backing: 4 yards

Batting: 71″ × 71″

Binding: ⅞ yard red (½″ finished width)

Cutting

To make templates for cutting, use Patterns 1 and 2 (page 78).

White

- Cut 17 strips 6½″ × width of fabric.

  Subcut 7 strips into 40 squares 6½″ × 6½″.

    Subcut 36 squares into frames using Template 2. Leave 4 squares uncut.

  Subcut 4 strips into 12 rectangles 6½″ × 12½″.

  Set aside the remaining 6 strips for the border.

- Cut 3 strips 6″ × width of fabric.

  Subcut into 18 squares 6″ × 6″.

Yellow

- Cut 4 strips 3″ × width of fabric.

  Subcut into 50 squares 3″ × 3″.

Red

- Cut 3 strips 6″ × width of fabric.

  Subcut into 18 squares 6″ × 6″.

- Cut 4 strips 3″ × width of fabric.

  Subcut into 50 squares 3″ × 3″.

- Cut 6 strips 2″ × width of fabric.

Backing

- Cut 2 pieces 71″ × width of fabric.

Binding

- Cut 7 red strips 3½″ × width of fabric. (This is for a ½″ finished binding. If you prefer a narrower binding, adjust accordingly.)

Construction

Seam allowances are ¼″. For detailed instructions on how to create this block, refer to Fan and Half-Square Triangle Variation (page 17).

Block Assembly

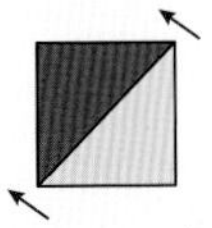

Make 100.

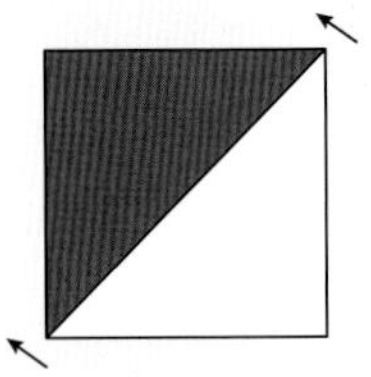

Make 36.

Red-and-Yellow Half-Square Triangle Units

Sew together 1 yellow square 3″ × 3″ and 1 red square 3″ × 3″ to make 2 half-square triangle units. Press the seams toward the red and trim the units to 2½″ × 2½″.

Red-and-White Half-Square Triangle Units

Sew together 1 white square 6″ × 6″ and 1 red square 6″ × 6″ to make 2 half-square triangle units. Press the seams toward the red.

Block A

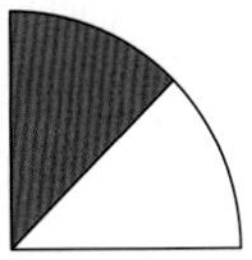

Block A quarter-circle cutting

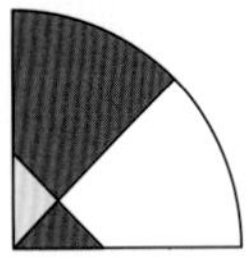

Make 20.

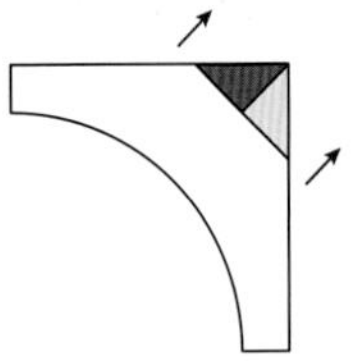

Make 20.

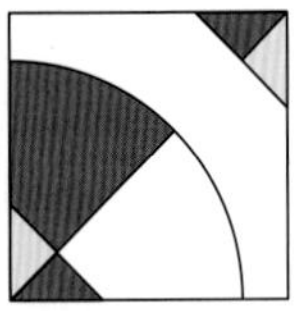

Make 20.

1. Subcut 20 red-and-white half-square triangle units into quarter-circles using Template 1. Orient the red and white as shown in the Block A quarter-circle cutting diagram.

2. Make a corner triangle by sewing together 1 red-and-yellow half-square triangle unit and 1 unit created in Step 1. Wait to press the seam.

3. Make a corner triangle by sewing together 1 red-and-yellow half-square triangle unit and a white frame piece. Press the seam toward the corner triangle.

4. Sew together the frame units and the quarter-circle units to create the block. Press the seams in one direction for 10 blocks and in the opposite direction for the other 10 blocks.

5. Arrange 4 blocks from Step 4 to make a large block, pairing blocks that have the seams pressed in opposite directions for nesting. Sew each side-by-side pair and press the seams in opposite directions for nesting as shown in the Block A assembly diagram. Then sew together 2 pairs to complete a block, pressing the horizontal seam toward the top of the block.

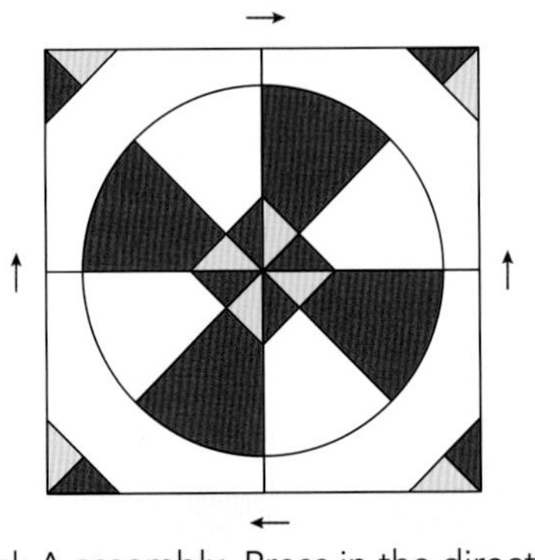

Block A assembly. Press in the direction of the arrows. Make 5.

Block B

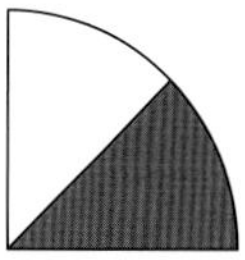

Block B quarter-circle cutting

1. Subcut 16 red-and-white half-square triangle units into quarter-circles using Template 1. Orient the red and white as shown in the Block B quarter-circle cutting diagram.

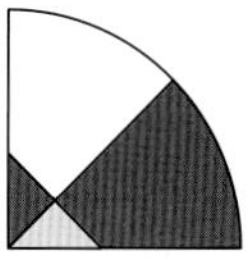

Make 16.

2. Make a corner triangle by sewing together 1 red-and-yellow half-square triangle unit and 1 unit created in Step 1. Wait to press the seam.

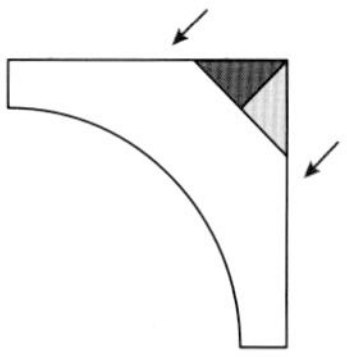

Make 16.

3. Make a corner triangle by sewing together 1 red-and-yellow half-square triangle unit and a white frame piece. Press the seam toward the frame.

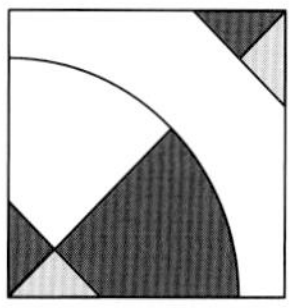

Make 16.

4. Sew together the frame and quarter-circle units. Press the seams in one direction for 8 blocks and in the opposite direction for the other 8 blocks.

5. Arrange 4 blocks from Step 4 to make a large block, pairing blocks that have the seams pressed in opposite directions for nesting. Sew each side-by-side pair and press the seams in opposite directions for nesting as shown in the Block B assembly diagram. Then sew together 2 pairs to complete a block, pressing the horizontal seam toward the bottom of the block.

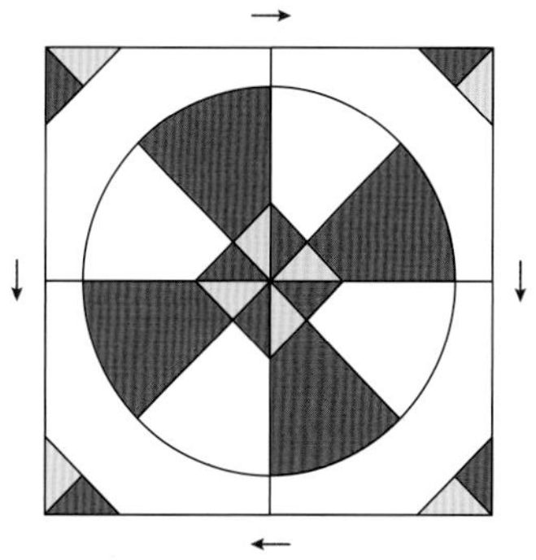

Block B assembly. Press in the direction of the arrows. Make 4.

Quilt Construction

1. Arrange the blocks as shown in the *Test Pattern* assembly diagram. If necessary, rotate the blocks so that the seams nest.

2. Sew the blocks together in rows, always pressing toward Block A.

3. Sew the rows together. Press the seams as you wish.

Test Pattern assembly

Borders

Pieced Inner Border

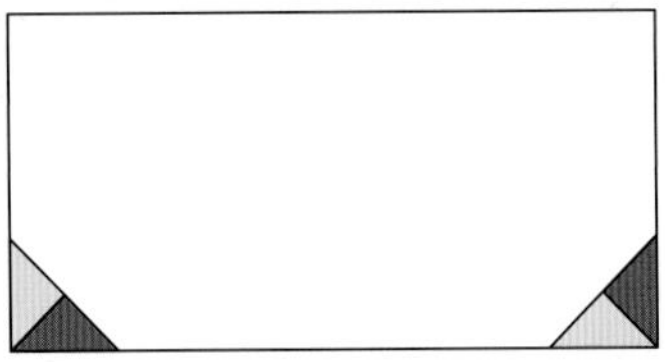

Make 12.

1. Sew together 1 white rectangle 6½″ × 12½″ and 2 red-and-yellow half-square triangle units to make the corner triangles. Press the seams open.

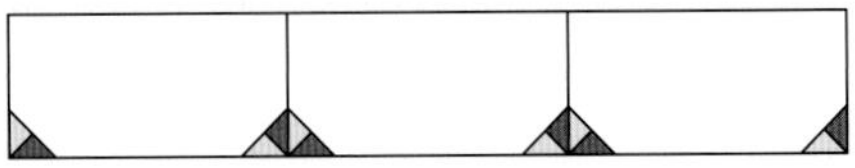

Make 4 border units.

2. Sew together 3 of these units along the 6½″ sides. Wait to press the seams. This is a border block unit.

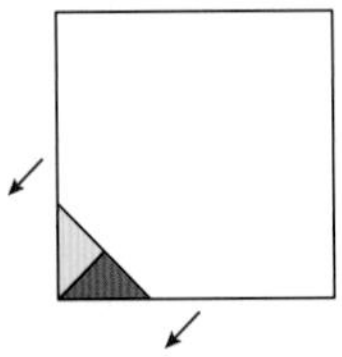

Make 4.

3. Sew 2 border block units to the sides of the quilt. Press the border block seams in the opposite direction of the matching seams in the quilt so that they nest. Press the long seam toward the outer border.

4. Make a corner triangle by sewing together 1 white square 6½″ × 6½″ and 1 red-and-yellow half-square triangle unit. Press the seam toward the corner triangle.

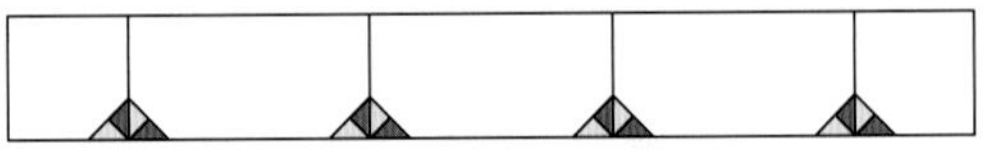

Make 2.

5. Sew 2 of these corner block units to the ends of the remaining border block units. Press the border block seams so that they nest with the seams in the body of the quilt. Attach these border strips to the top and bottom of the quilt.

Red Inner Border

1. Trim the selvages from the 6 red strips 2″ × width of fabric and stitch them together on the diagonal; subcut into 2 strips 2″ × 48½″ and 2 strips 2″ × 51½″.

2. Sew the strips 2″ × 48½″ to the sides of the quilt. Press the seams toward the red border.

3. Sew the strips 2″ × 51½″ to the top and bottom of the quilt. Press the seams toward the red border.

White Border

1. Trim the selvages from the 6 white strips 6½″ × width of fabric and stitch them on the diagonal; subcut into 2 strips 6½″ × 51½″ and 2 strips 6½″ × 63½″.

2. Sew the 2 strips 6½″ × 51½″ to the sides of the quilt. Press the seams toward the red border.

3. Sew the 2 strips 6½″ × 63½″ to the top and bottom of the quilt. Press the seams toward the red border.

Finishing

1. Trim the selvage edges of the 2 backing pieces and sew them together along the 71″ sides.

2. Layer, baste, and quilt as desired.

3. Sew together the 3½″-wide binding strips on the diagonal.

4. Attach the binding to the quilt with a ½″ seam allowance using your preferred method.

TILE FLOOR

Finished blocks: 6″ × 6″, 12″ × 12″ • **Finished quilt:** 60″ × 60″

*Blues and golds create this colorful design inspired by a tile floor. I used Marcia Derse's collections **Palette, Mosaic,** and **Botanical** and Melanie Testa's collection **Meadowlark,** both from Windham Fabrics. Swap the cream and gold backgrounds for white and black, throw in some vibrant colors, and you will get a harlequin quilt. Or tone it down with tans, browns, and taupes.*

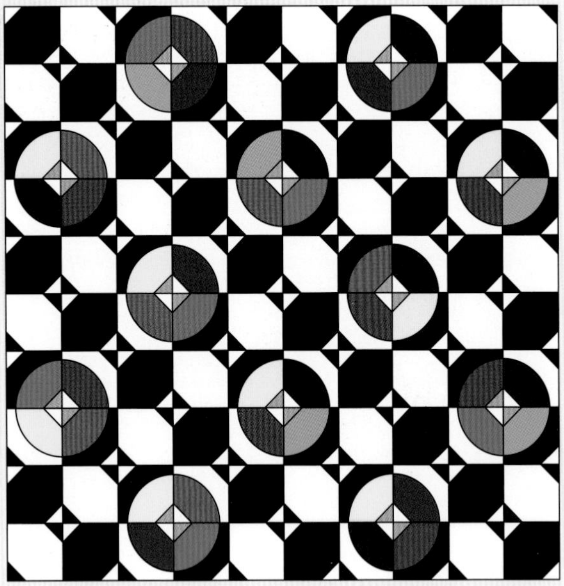

Using a variety of colors with a black-and-white background can make this quilt glow. This would be a great way to use small-scale prints.

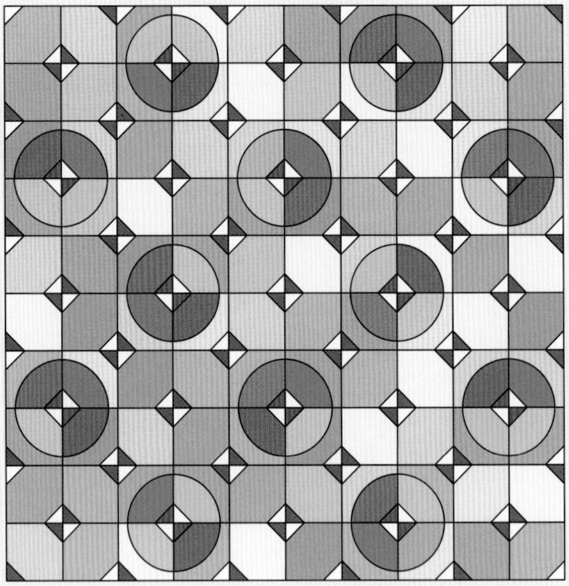

Using neutral tones gives the quilt a calm feeling.

DESIGNER'S TIP

To create your own colorway, start by selecting fabric for the circles. Choose two similar values of the same color and then select background fabrics that will make your circles stand out. The background colors should vary slightly in value. Finally, pick a color for the small triangles—you want something that will give a little pop and sparkle to your quilt as the yellow does in Test Pattern.

Materials

These fabrics are tonal solids that resemble hand dyes; they have a subtle variation in color.

Cream: 2¼ yards

Gold: 1⅞ yards

Dark blue: 1⅛ yards

Medium blue: ⅞ yard

Teal: ¼ yard

Backing: 3⅞ yards

Batting: 68″ × 68″

Binding: ⅞ yard gold (½″ finished width)

Cutting

To make templates for cutting, use Patterns 1 and 2 (page 78).

Cream

- Cut 9 strips 6½″ × width of fabric.

  Subcut into 50 squares 6½″ × 6½″.

  Set aside 26 squares 6½″ × 6½″.

  Subcut the remaining 24 squares into frames using Template 2.

  From the quarter-circle waste fabric:

  Cut 24 squares 2½″ × 2½″.

- Cut 5 strips 2½″ × width of fabric.

  Subcut into 76 squares 2½″ × 2½″ for a total of 100.

Gold

- Cut 9 strips 6½″ × width of fabric.

  Subcut into 50 squares 6½″ × 6½″.

  Set aside 26 squares 6½″ × 6½″.

  Subcut the remaining 24 squares into frames using Template 2.

Dark blue

- Cut 4 strips 5½″ × width of fabric.

  Subcut into 24 quarter-circles using Template 1.

- Cut 5 strips 2½″ × width of fabric.

  Subcut into 76 squares 2½″ × 2½″.

Medium blue

- Cut 4 strips 5½″ × width of fabric.

  Subcut into 24 quarter-circles using Template 1.

Teal

- Cut 2 strips 2½″ × width of fabric.

  Subcut into 24 squares 2½″ × 2½″.

Backing

- Cut 2 pieces 68″ × width of fabric.

Binding

- Cut 7 strips 3½″ × width of fabric. (This is for a ½″ finished binding. If you prefer a narrower binding, adjust accordingly.)

Construction

Seam allowances are ¼″. For detailed instructions on how to create these blocks, refer to Corner Triangle Variation (page 14).

Block Assembly

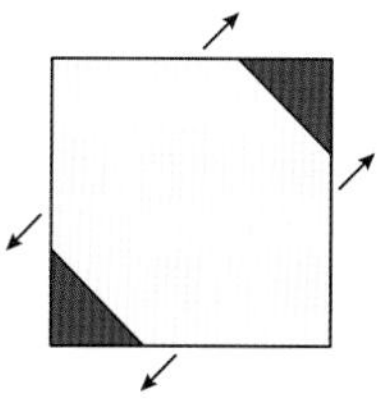

Make 26.

Block A

Sew 2 dark blue squares 2½″ × 2½″ onto the opposite corners of 1 cream square 6½″ × 6½″, making half-square triangles. Trim the seam to ¼″ and press toward the blue.

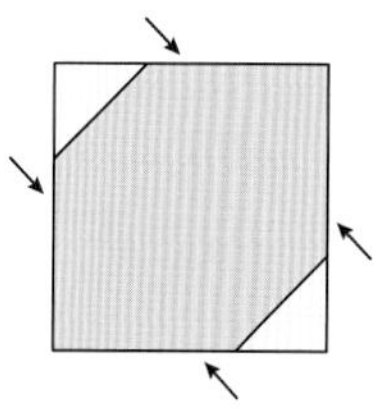

Make 26.

Block B

Sew 2 cream squares 2½″ × 2½″ onto the opposite corners of 1 gold square 6½″ × 6½″, making half-square triangles. Trim the seam to ¼″ and press toward the gold.

Block AB

1. Sew together 1 Block A and 1 Block B. Press toward Block B.

2. Sew together 2 units from Step 1 to make a Block AB. Press the seam up.

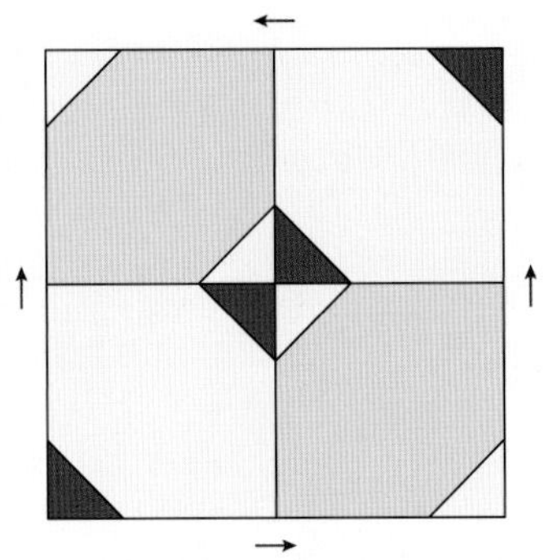

Block AB: Make 13.

Block C

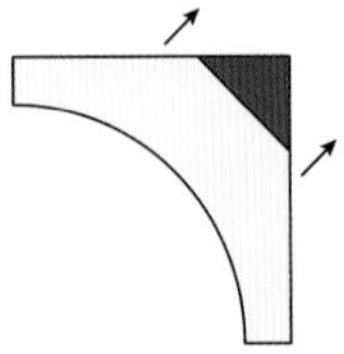

Make 24.

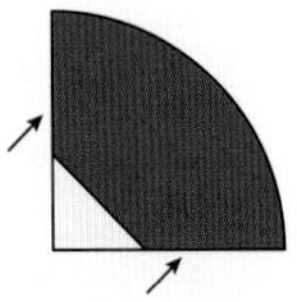

Make 24.

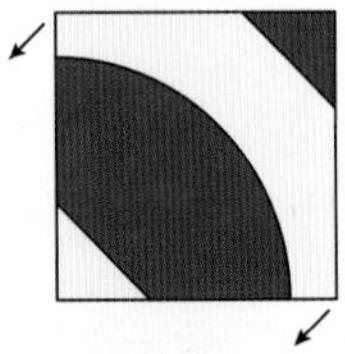

Make 24.

1. Sew 1 dark blue square 2½″ × 2½″ to 1 cream frame piece, making a corner triangle. Trim the seam to ¼″ and press toward the blue.

2. Sew 1 cream 2½″ × 2½″ square to 1 dark blue quarter-circle piece, making a corner triangle. Trim the seam to ¼″ and press toward the blue.

3. Sew together a frame and a quarter-circle unit from Steps 1 and 2. Press the seam toward the blue quarter-circle unit.

Block D

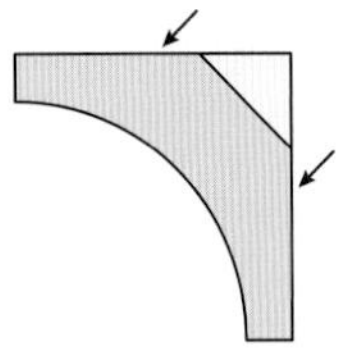

Make 24.

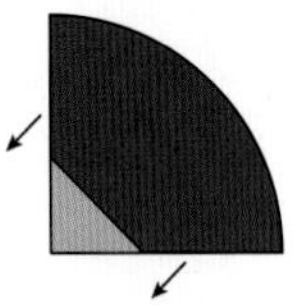

Make 24.

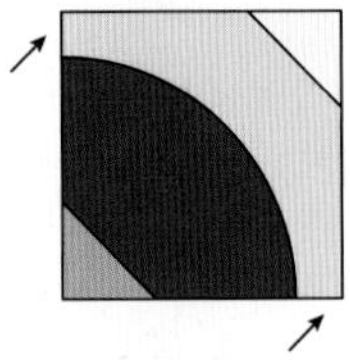

Make 24.

1. Sew 1 cream square 2½″ × 2½″ onto 1 gold frame piece, making a corner triangle. Trim the seam to ¼″ and press toward the gold.

2. Sew 1 teal square 2½″ × 2½″ onto 1 medium blue quarter-circle piece, making a corner triangle. Trim the seam to ¼″ and press toward the teal.

3. Sew together a frame and a quarter-circle unit from Steps 1 and 2. Press the seam toward the gold.

Block CD

1. Sew together 1 Block C and 1 Block D. Press toward Block D.

2. Sew together 2 units from Step 1 to make a Block CD. Press the seam down.

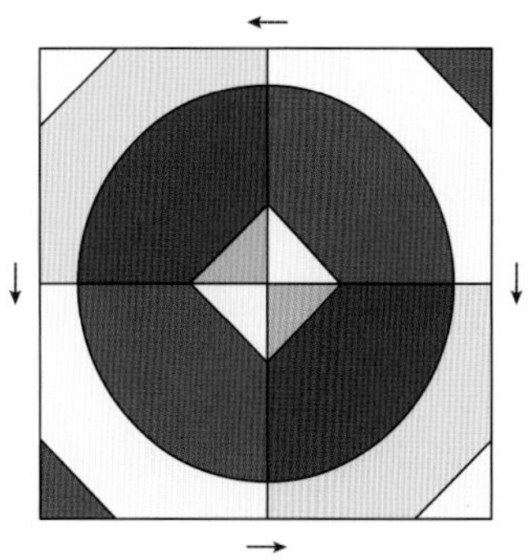

Block CD: Make 12.

Quilt Construction

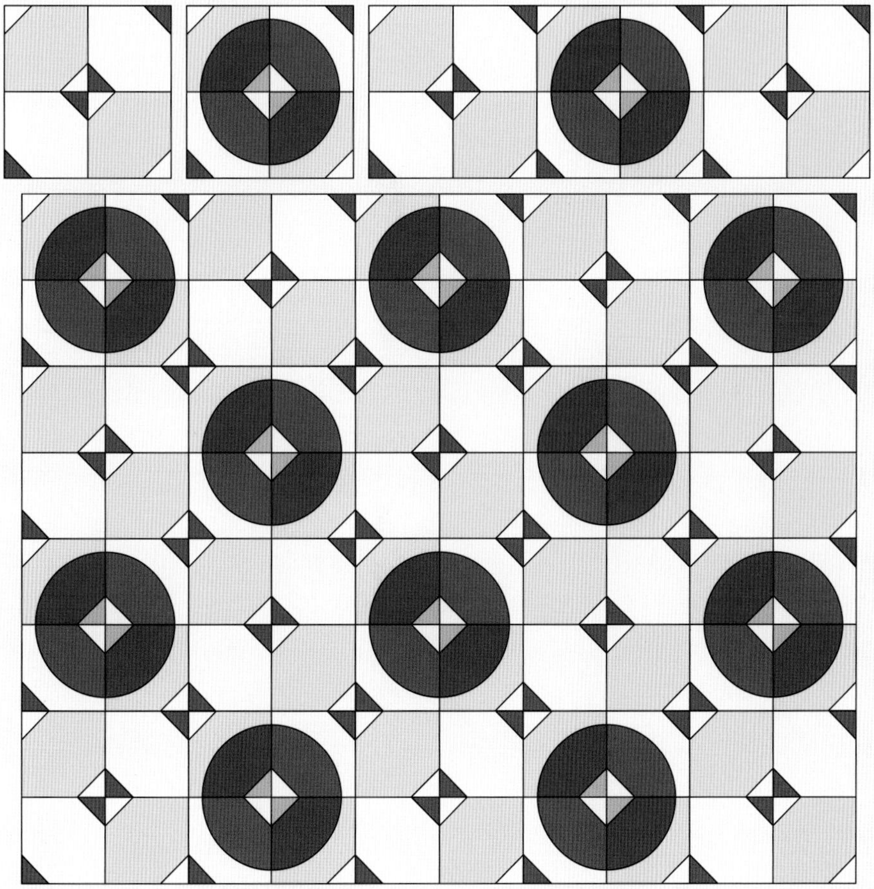

Tile Floor assembly

1. Arrange the blocks as shown in the *Tile Floor* assembly diagram. Rotate the blocks so that the seams nest.

2. Sew the blocks together into rows. Press the seams toward Block AB.

3. Sew the rows together. Press the seams as you wish.

Finishing

1. Trim the selvage edges of the 2 backing pieces and join together along the 68″ sides.

2. Layer, baste, and quilt as desired.

3. Sew the 3½″-wide binding strips together on the diagonal.

4. Attach the binding to the quilt with a ½″ seam allowance using your preferred method.

NIGHTFALL

Finished block: 6″ × 6″ • **Finished quilt:** 89″ × 89″

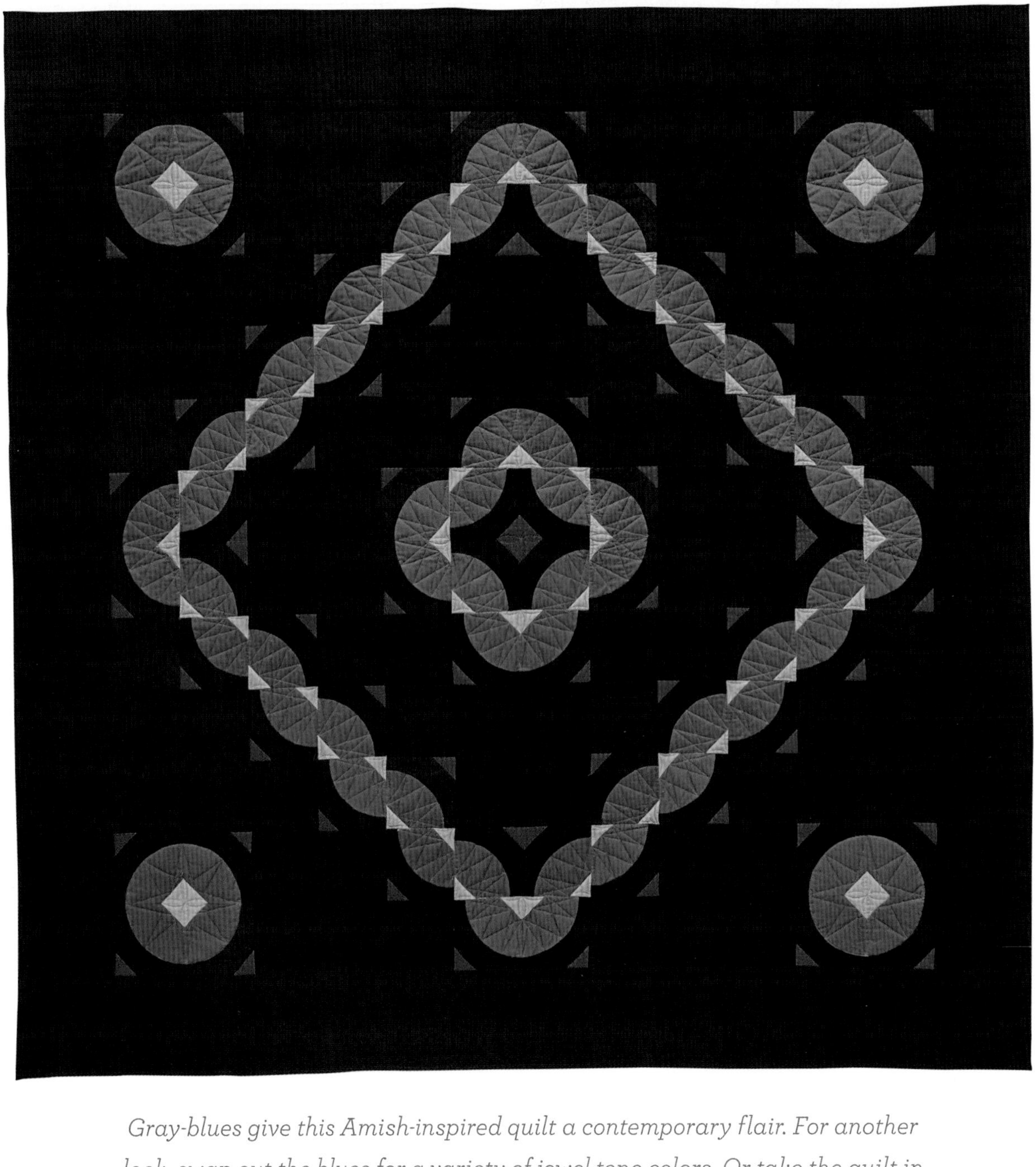

Gray-blues give this Amish-inspired quilt a contemporary flair. For another look, swap out the blues for a variety of jewel-tone colors. Or take the quilt in the opposite direction and use a light background color for your quilt..

Elegant jewel tones replace the blues and pop against a black background.

White replaces the black, and rich blues give this pattern a crisp and bright look.

Materials

Black: 7½ yards

Dark gray-blue: 1⅞ yards

Medium gray-blue: ½ yard

Fuchsia: ½ yard

Backing: 8⅛ yards

Batting: 97″ × 97″

Binding: 1⅛ yards black (½″ finished width)

Cutting

To make templates for cutting, use Patterns 1 and 2 (page 78).

Black

- Cut 18 strips 6½″ × width of fabric.

  Subcut 3 strips into 8 rectangles 6½″ × 12½″.

  Subcut 15 strips into 88 squares 6½″ × 6½″.

    Subcut 72 squares 6½″ × 6½″ into frames using Template 2.

- Cut 4 strips 12½″ × width of fabric.

  Subcut into 10 squares 12½″ × 12½″.

- Cut 2 strips parallel to the selvage 9″ × 72½″.

- Cut 2 strips parallel to the selvage 9″ × 89½″.

Dark gray-blue

- Cut 11 strips 5½″ × width of fabric.

  Subcut into 72 quarter-circles using Template 1.

Medium gray-blue

- Cut 5 strips 2½″ × width of fabric.

  Subcut into 72 squares 2½″ × 2½″.

Fuchsia

- Cut 5 strips 2½″ × width of fabric.

  Subcut into 72 squares 2½″ × 2½″.

Backing

- Cut 3 pieces 97″ × width of fabric.

Binding

- Cut 10 strips 3½″ × width of fabric. (This is for a ½″ finished binding. If you prefer a narrower binding, adjust accordingly.)

Construction

Seam allowances are ¼″. For detailed instructions on how to create this block, refer to Corner Triangle Variation (page 14).

Block Assembly

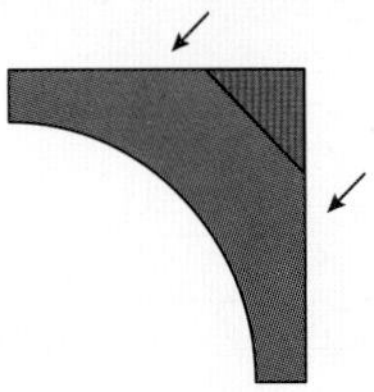

Make 72.

1. Sew 1 fuchsia 2½″ × 2½″ square onto 1 black frame piece to make a corner triangle. Press the seam toward the black.

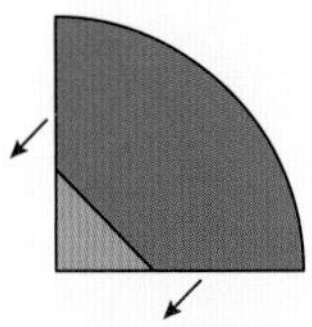

Make 72.

2. Sew 1 medium blue square 2½″ × 2½″ onto 1 dark gray-blue quarter-circle piece to make a corner triangle. Press the seam toward the corner triangle.

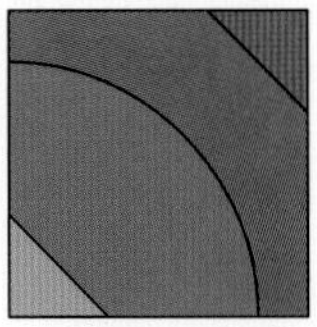

Make 72.

3. Sew together the units made in Steps 1 and 2. Wait to press the seam.

Unit Assembly

When constructing the units, press all seams in the direction indicated by the arrows on the diagrams so that the seams nest.

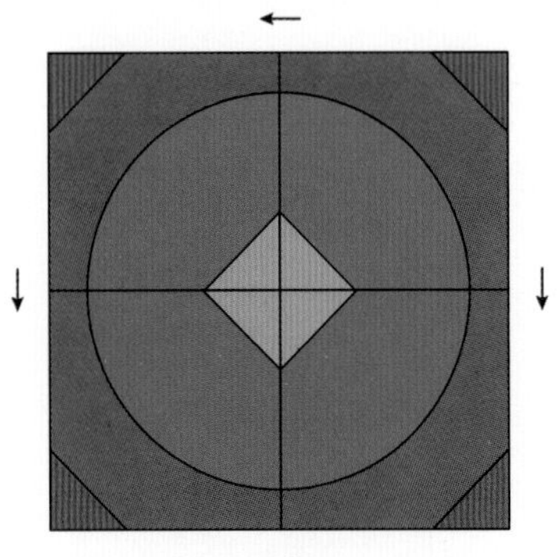

Unit A: Make 4.

Unit A

Sew together 4 blocks to make Unit A.

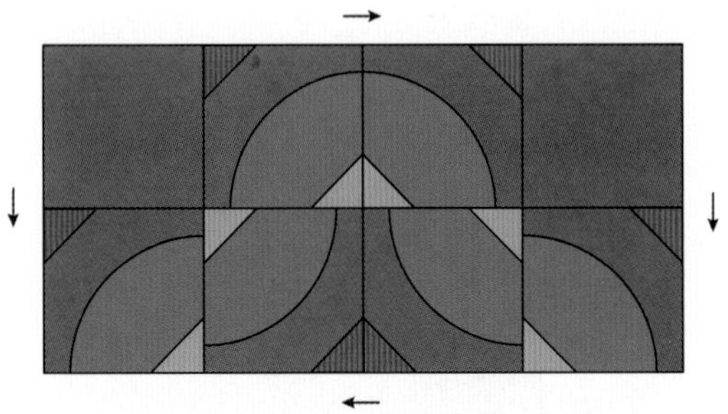

Unit B: Make 2.

Unit B

Sew together 6 blocks and 2 black squares 6½″ × 6½″ to make Unit B.

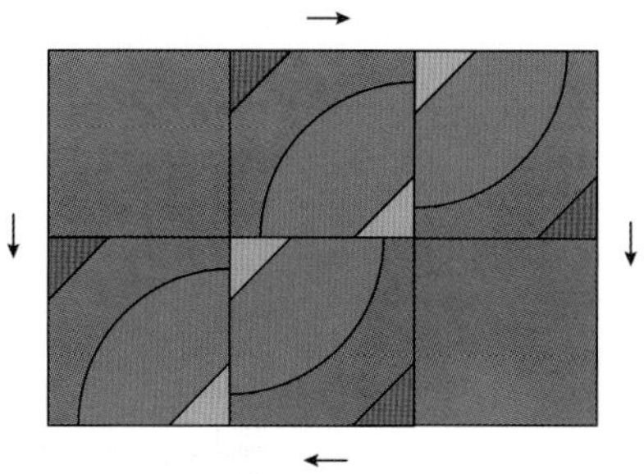

Unit C1: Make 2.

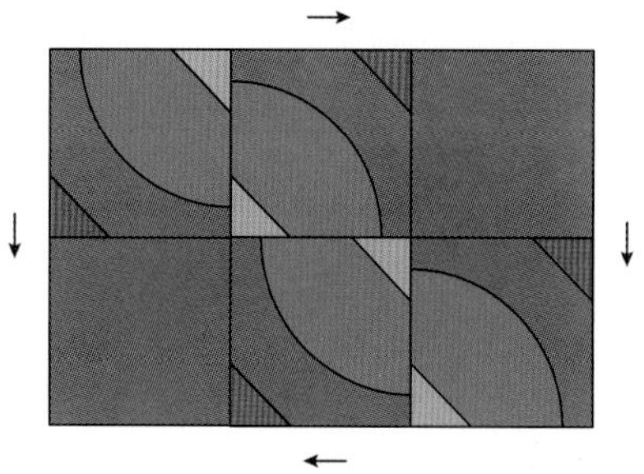

Unit C2: Make 2.

Unit C1

Sew together 4 blocks and 2 black squares 6½″ × 6½″ to make Unit C1.

Unit C2

Sew together 4 blocks and 2 black squares 6½″ × 6½″ to make Unit C2.

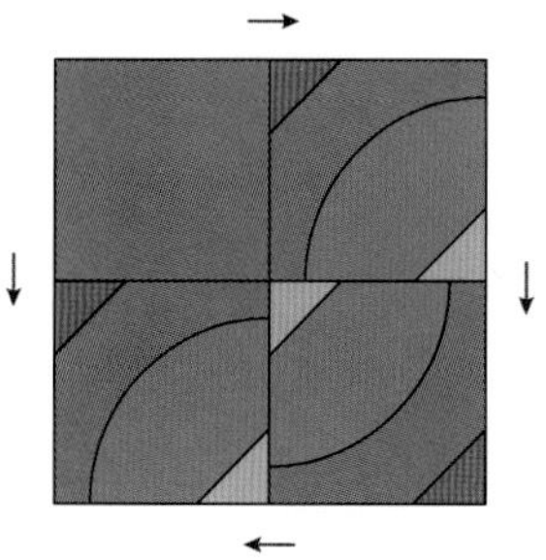

Unit D1: Make 2.

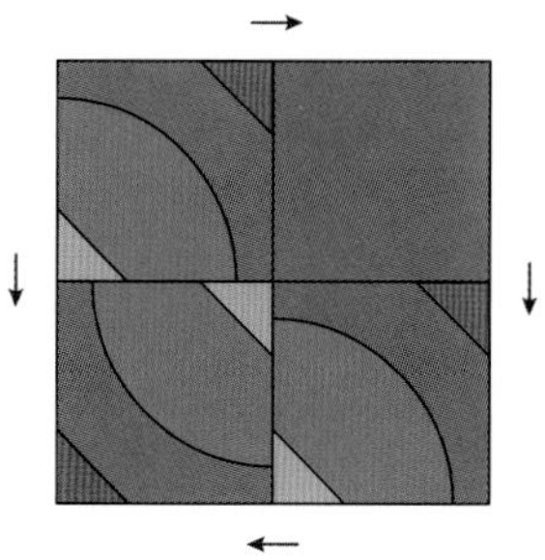

Unit D2: Make 2.

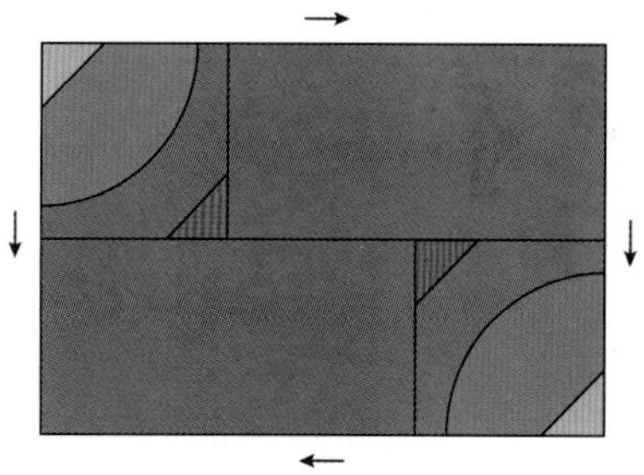

Unit E1: Make 2.

Unit D1

Sew together 3 blocks and 1 black square 6½″ × 6½″ to make Unit D1.

Unit D2

Sew together 3 blocks and 1 black square 6½″ × 6½″ to make Unit D2.

Unit E1

Sew together 2 blocks and 2 black rectangles 6½″ × 12½″ to make Unit E1.

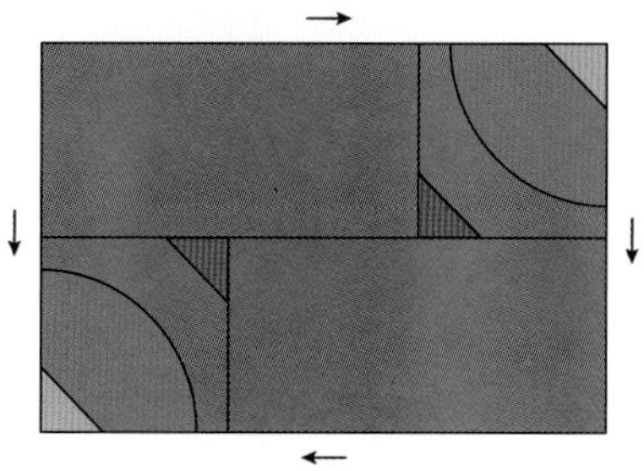

Unit E2: Make 2.

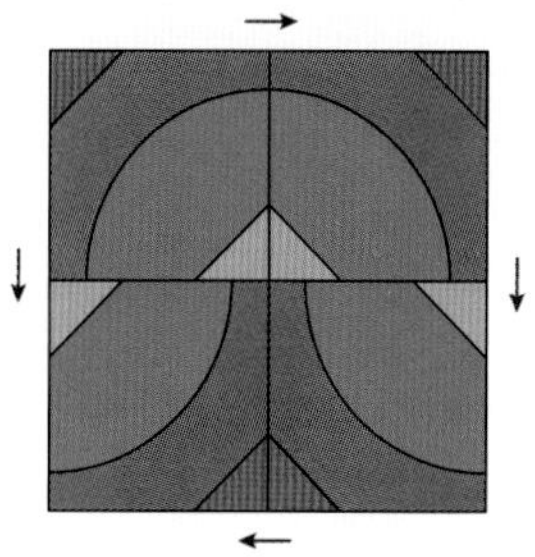

Unit F: Make 2.

Unit E2

Sew together 2 blocks and 2 black rectangles 6½″ × 12½″ to make Unit E2.

Unit F

Sew together 4 blocks to make Unit F.

Row Assembly

When constructing the rows, press all seams in the direction indicated by the arrows on the diagrams so that the seams nest.

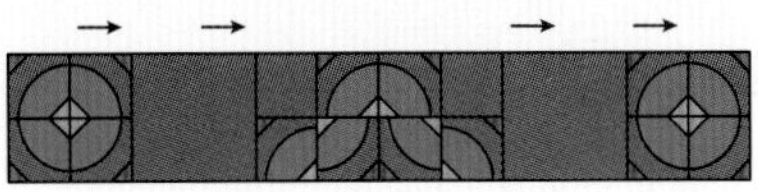

Row 1: Make 2.

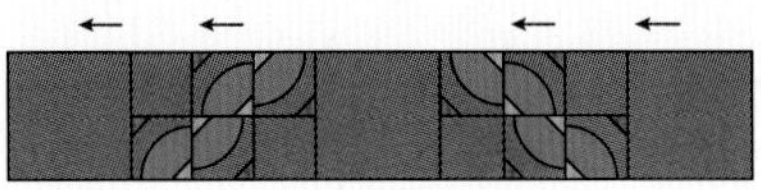

Row 2: Make 2.

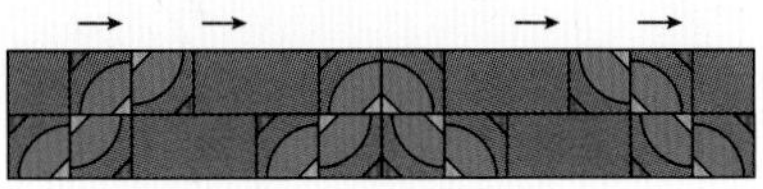

Row 3: Make 2.

Row 1

Sew together 2 Units A, 1 Unit B, and 2 black squares 12½″ × 12½″ to make Row 1.

Row 2

Sew together 1 Unit C1, 1 Unit C2, and 3 black squares 12½″ × 12½″ to make Row 2.

Row 3

Sew together 1 Unit D1, 1 Unit E1, 1 Unit F, 1 Unit E2, and 1 Unit D2 to make Row 3.

Quilt Construction

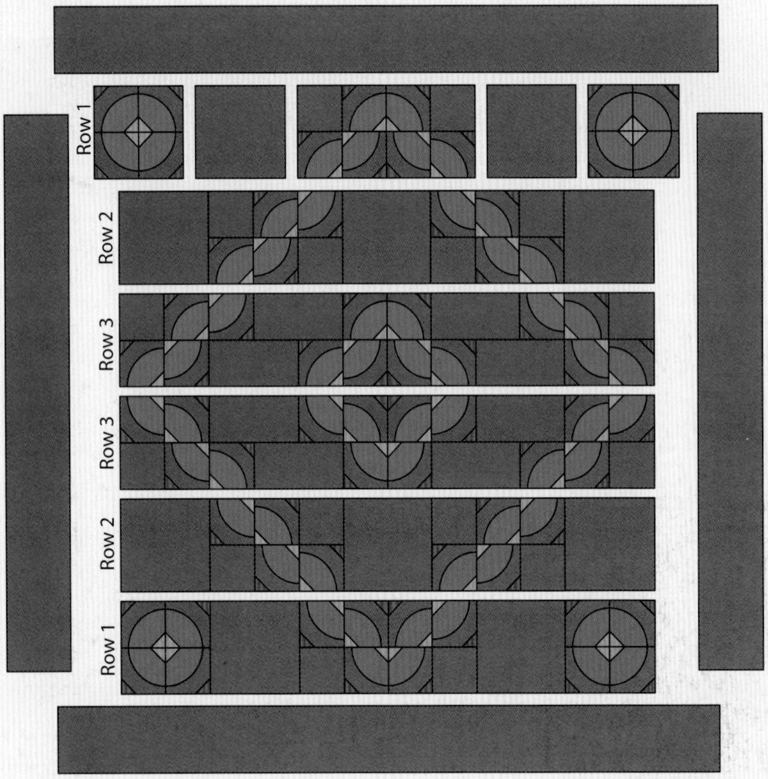

Nightfall assembly

1. Arrange the rows as shown in the *Nightfall* assembly diagram.
2. Sew the rows together. Press the seams as you wish.

Borders

1. Sew 2 black strips 9″ × 72½″ to the sides of quilt. Press the seams toward the black border.
2. Sew 2 black strips 9″ × 89½″ to the top and bottom of the quilt. Press the seams toward the black border.

Finishing

1. Trim the selvage edges of the 3 backing pieces and join together along the 97″ sides.
2. Layer, baste, and quilt as desired.
3. Sew the 3½″-wide binding strips together on the diagonal.
4. Attach the binding to the quilt with a ½″ seam allowance using your preferred method.

ABSTRACT

Finished blocks: 6″ × 6″, 12″ × 12″ • **Finished quilt:** 60″ × 60″

Charcoal, black, and cream fabrics from Pepper Cory's ***Peppered Cottons*** *collection for Studio E Fabrics give* ***Abstract*** *a very monochromatic look. If you want more color but like the quiet look, add some warmer neutrals. Or go with a dark background and lively colors for a vivid look.*

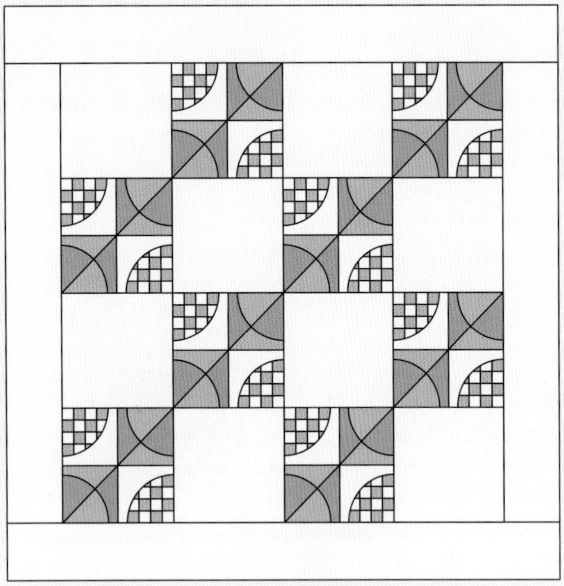

The cream background remains, but muted colors are added in place of the grays and browns.

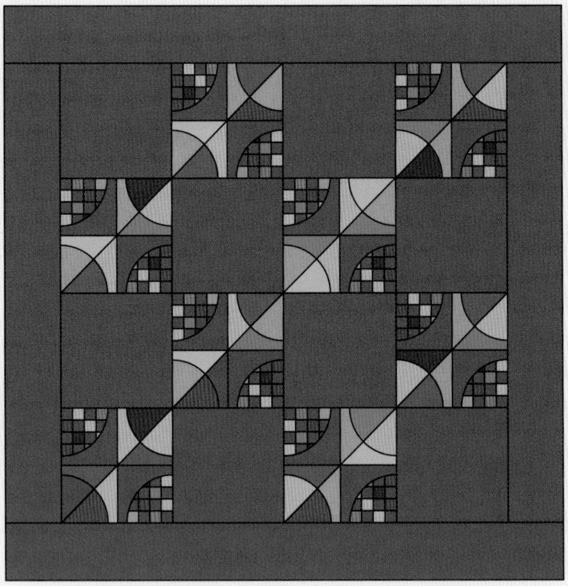

A slightly darker background color and some brighter hues create a lively quilt.

Materials

Cream: 3½ yards

Medium gray: ⅜ yard

Dark gray: 1 yard

Brown: 1 yard

Backing: 3⅞ yards

Batting: 68″ × 68″

Binding: ⅞ yard cream (½″ finished width)

Cutting

To make templates for cutting, use Patterns 1 and 2 (page 78).

Cream

- Cut 6 strips 1¾″ × width of fabric.
- Cut 3 strips 12½″ × width of fabric.

  Subcut into 8 squares 12½″ × 12½″.
- Cut 2 strips parallel to the selvage 6½″ × 48½″.
- Cut 2 strips parallel to the selvage 6½″ × 60½″.
- From the yardage remaining from the parallel cuts, cut 16 squares 6½″ × 6½″.

  Subcut into 16 frames using Template 2.

Medium gray

- Cut 6 strips 1¾″ × width of fabric.

Dark gray

- Cut 2 strips 6″ × width of fabric.

  Subcut into 8 squares 6″ × 6″.
- Cut 2 strips 7″ × width of fabric.

  Subcut into 8 squares 7″ × 7″.

Brown

- Cut 2 strips 6″ × width of fabric.

  Subcut into 8 squares 6″ × 6″.
- Cut 2 strips 7″ × width of fabric.

  Subcut into 8 squares 7″ × 7″.

Backing

- Cut 2 strips 68″ × width of fabric.

Binding

- Cut 7 strips 3½″ × width of fabric. (This is for a ½″ finished binding. If you prefer a narrower binding, adjust accordingly.)

Construction

Seam allowances are ¼″.

Block Assembly

Block A

For detailed instructions on how to create this block, refer to Fan Variation (page 15).

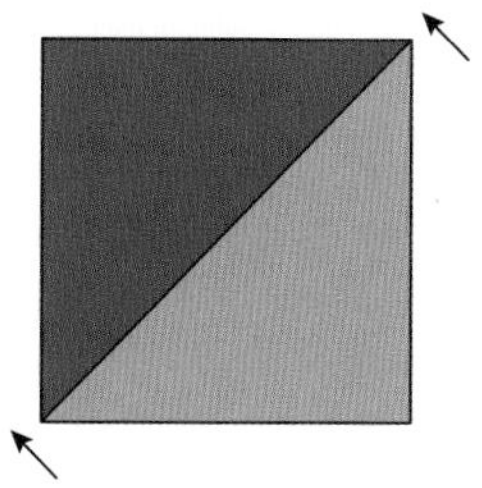

Make 16.

1. Sew together 1 brown square 6″ × 6″ and 1 black square 6″ × 6″ to make 2 half-square triangle units. Press the seams toward the black. Trim the units to 5½″ × 5½″.

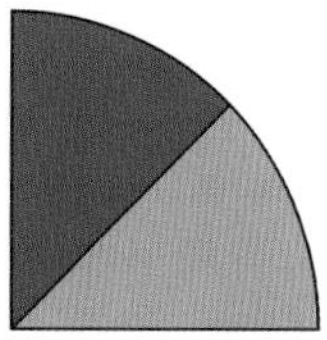

Block A quarter-circle cutting

2. Subcut the units made in Step 1 into quarter-circles using Template 1. Orient the black and brown as shown in the Block A quarter-circle cutting diagram.

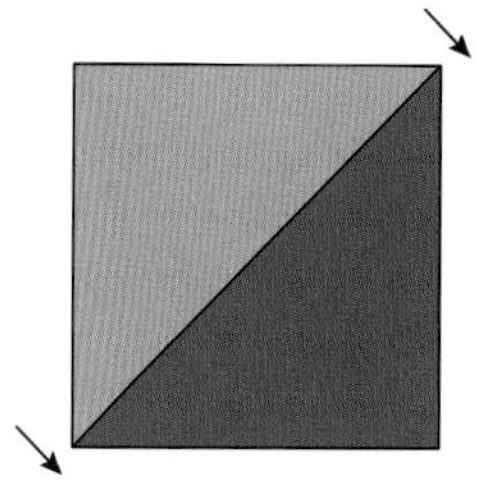

Make 16.

3. Sew together 1 brown square 7″ × 7″ and 1 black square 7″ × 7″ to make 2 half-square triangle units. Press the seams toward the black. Trim the units to 6½″ × 6½″.

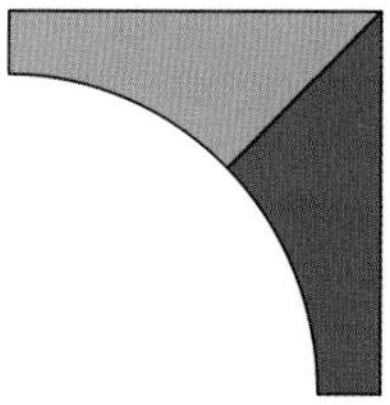

Block A frame cutting

4. Subcut the half-square triangle units made in Step 3 into frames using Template 2. Orient the black and brown as shown in the Block A frame cutting diagram.

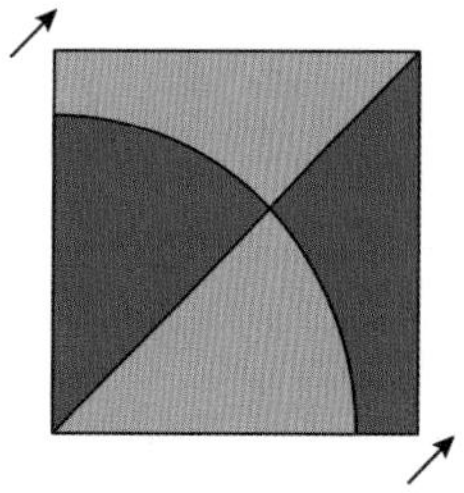

Block A: Make 16.

5. Sew together the units created in Steps 2 and 4 as shown the in the Block A diagram. Press the seam toward the frame.

Block B

For detailed instructions on how to create this block, refer to Sixteen-Patch Variation (page 18).

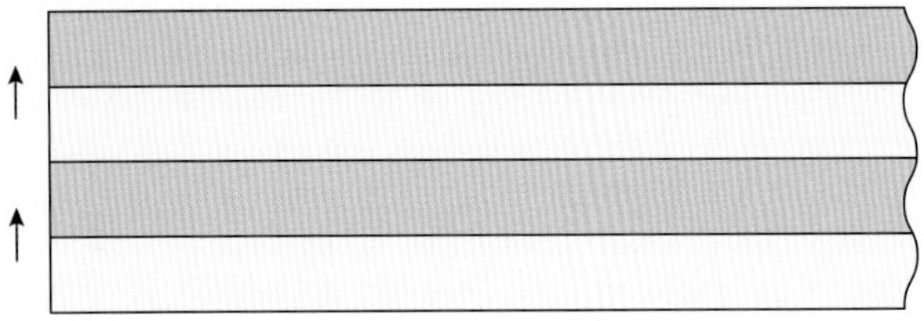

Make 3.

Make 64.

1. Sew a strip set using 2 cream strips 1¾″ × width of fabric and 2 light gray strips 1½″ × width of fabric. Press the seams toward the light gray.

2. Subcut the strip sets into 64 rectangles 1¾″ × 5½″.

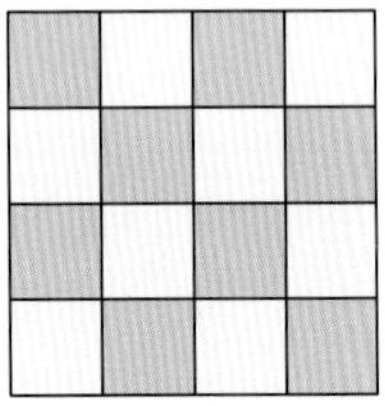

Make 16.

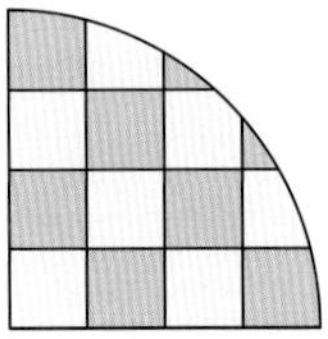

Block B quarter-circle cutting

3. Sew together 4 rectangles from Step 2 to make a Sixteen-Patch block. Press the seams as you wish.

4. Subcut the blocks into quarter-circles using Template 1. Make sure that the cream square is in the bottom corner of each quarter-circle unit.

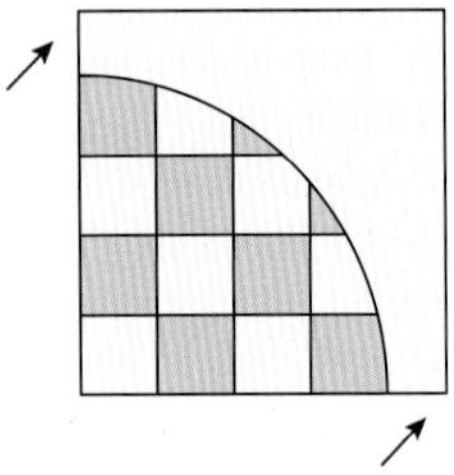

Block B: Make 16.

5. Sew together the Step 4 quarter-circle units and the cream frame units. Press the seam toward the frame.

Block AB

Sew together 2 Blocks A and 2 Blocks B. Press the seams so that they nest.

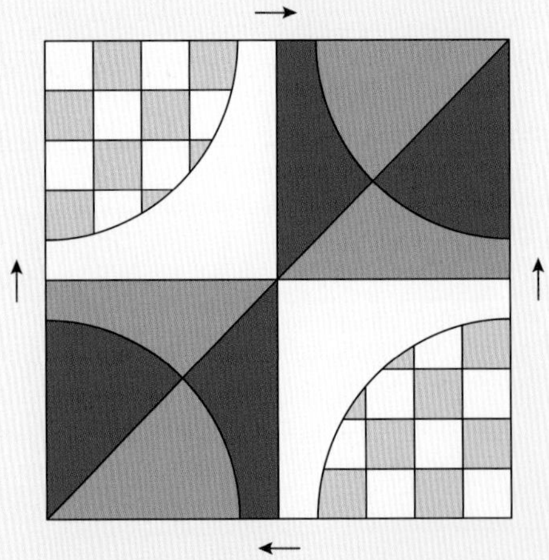

Block AB: Make 8.

Quilt Construction

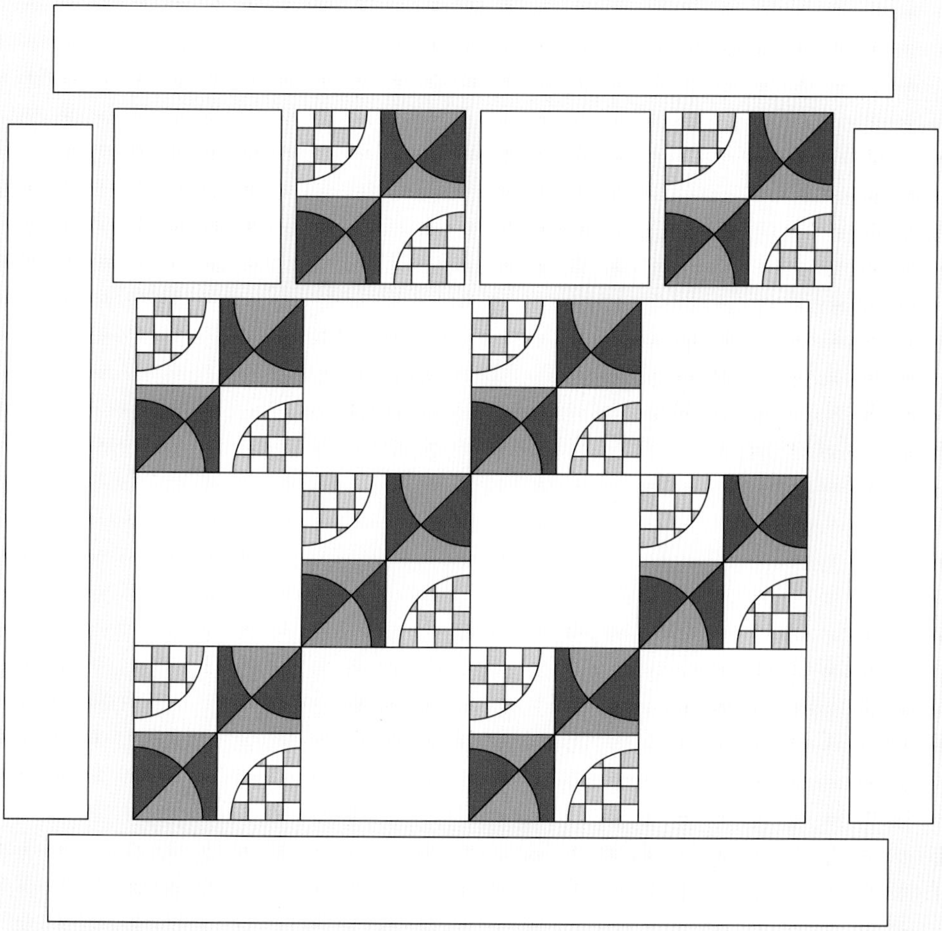

Abstract assembly

1. Arrange the blocks as shown in the *Abstract* assembly diagram.

2. Sew the blocks together into rows. Press the seams toward the cream blocks.

3. Sew the rows together. Press the seams as you wish.

Borders

1. Sew 2 cream strips 6½″ × 48½″ to the sides of the quilt. Press the seams toward the border.

2. Sew 2 cream strips parallel to the selvage 6½″ × 60½″. Press the seams toward the border.

Finishing

1. Trim the selvage edges of the 2 backing pieces and join together along the 68″ sides.

2. Layer, baste, and quilt as desired.

3. Sew together the 3½″-wide binding strips on the diagonal.

4. Attach the binding with a ½″ seam allowance using your preferred method.

SNAKE IN THE GRASS

Finished block: 6″ × 6″ • **Finished quilt:** 60″ × 60″

Slinky creatures slither through grass in this unusual layout that uses a Rail Fence pattern for the frame unit. The curvy blues, from Art Gallery Fabrics and Cotton + Steel by RJR Fabrics, pop against the lines of lime. Swap out the blues for yellows and oranges and you will have a citrus design that celebrates the tropics. Or switch out the lights for darks and the darks for lights to create a totally different look.

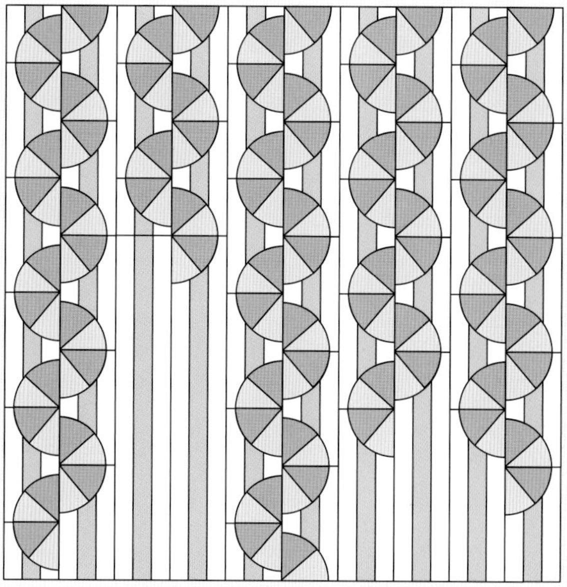

Add interest to the quilt by using the Fan Variation (page 15).

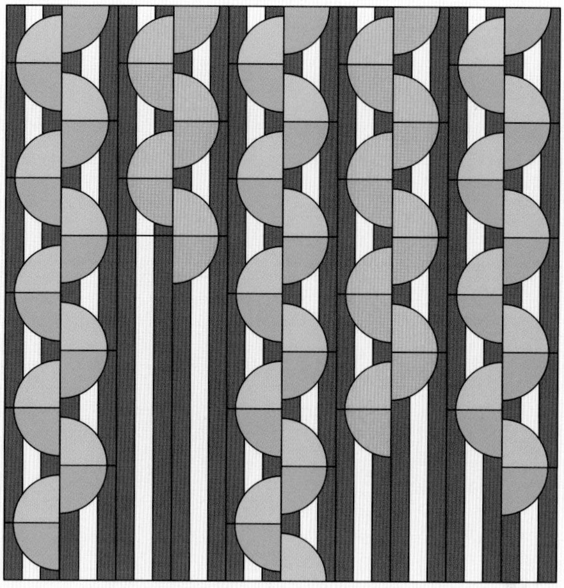

Reverse the values and the quilt takes on a totally different look.

DESIGNER'S TIP

You can easily enlarge Snake in the Grass *by adding more rows and making them longer. If you do, consider having some of the designs start at the bottom and go only partway up the quilt.*

Materials

For the dark blue fabrics, use solids, prints, tone-on-tone designs, or a mix.

White-and-gray small print: 2½ yards

Lime green: 1⅜ yards

Dark blues: 8 pieces, ½ yard of each

Backing: 3⅞ yards

Batting: 68″ × 68″

Binding: ⅞ yard white (½″ finished width)

Cutting

To make templates for cutting, use Patterns 1 and 2 (page 78).

White-and-gray small print

- Cut 34 strips 2½″ × width of fabric.

Lime green

- Cut 17 strips 2½″ × width of fabric.

Dark blues

From each piece:

- Cut 2 strips 5½″ × width of fabric.

  Subcut into 10 quarter-circles using Template 1.

Backing

- Cut 2 pieces 68″ × width of fabric.

Binding

- Cut 7 strips 3½″ × width of fabric. (This is for a ½″ finished binding. If you prefer a narrower binding, adjust accordingly.)

Construction

Seam allowances are ¼″. For detailed instructions on how to create this block, refer to Rail Fence Variation (page 18).

Block Assembly

Strip Sets

1. Sew 2 white-and-gray strips 2½″ × width of fabric to the opposite sides of 1 lime-green strip 2½″ × width of fabric. Press the seams open.

2. Subcut the strip sets into 2 rectangles 6½″ × 36½″, 1 rectangle 6½″ × 24½″, 2 rectangles 6½″ × 18½″, 35 rectangles 6½″ × 12½″, and 8 squares 6½″ × 6½″.

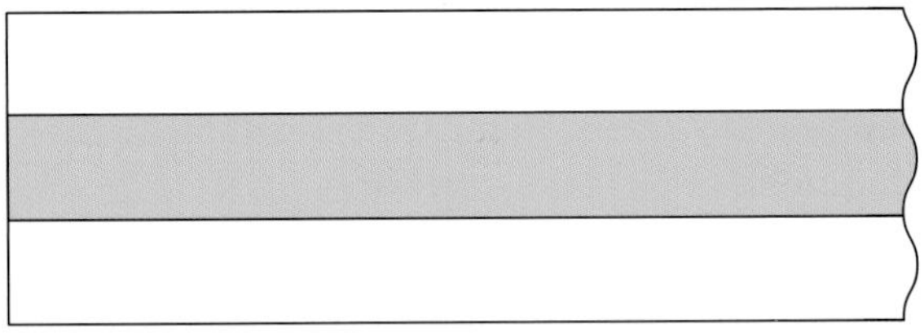

Make 17.

Frames

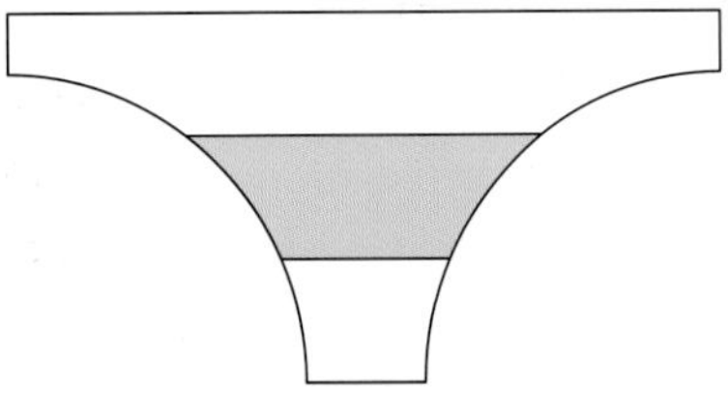

Make 33.

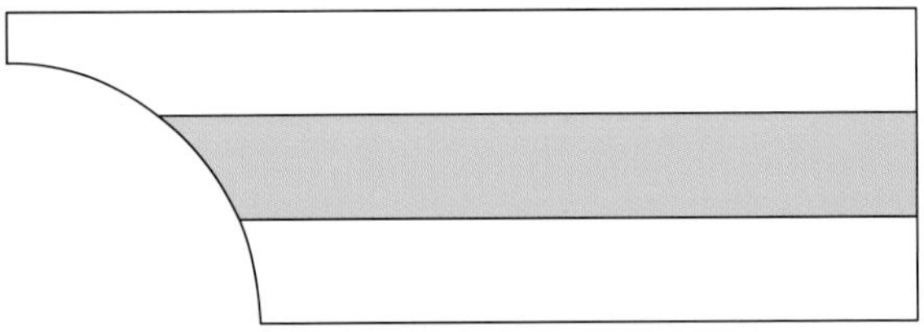

1. Subcut 33 of the strip-set rectangles 6½″ × 12½″ into frames using Template 2.

2. Subcut 1 strip-set piece 6½″ × 36½″, 1 strip-set piece 6½″ × 24½″, and 2 strip-set rectangles 6½″ × 12½″ into frames using Template 2.

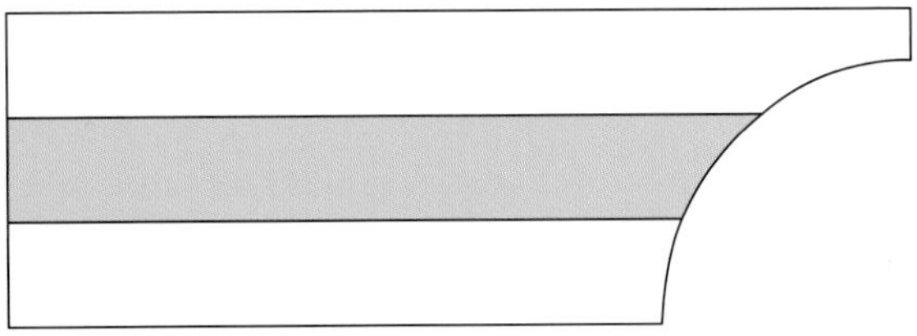

Make 2.

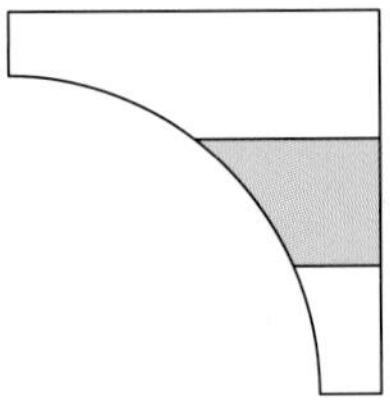

Make 5.

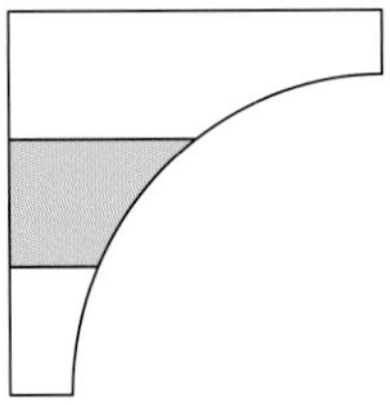

Make 3.

3. Subcut 2 strip-set rectangles 6½″ × 18½″ into frames using Template 2.

4. Subcut 5 strip-set squares 6½″ × 6½″ into frames using Template 2 as shown.

5. Subcut 3 strip-set squares 6½″ × 6½″ into frames using Template 2 as shown.

Quilt Construction

Snake in the Grass assembly

1. Arrange the frame units and the other rectangular strip-set units as shown in the *Snake in the Grass* assembly diagram. Next, randomly arrange the quarter-circle units, repositioning them until you are pleased with the design.

2. Remove the blocks one at a time and sew together the frames and quarter-circles. Return each block to its place as it is sewn. Press the seams of adjacent quarter-circle units in opposite directions for nesting.

3. Sew the quilt together in vertical columns. Press the seams in opposite directions from column to column so that the seams nest.

4. Sew the columns together. Press the seams as you wish.

Finishing

1. Trim the selvage edges of the 2 backing pieces and join together along the 68″ sides.

2. Layer, baste, and quilt as desired.

3. Sew together the 3½″-wide binding strips on the diagonal.

4. Attach the binding to the quilt with a ½″ seam allowance using your preferred method.

SHAKEN NOT STIRRED

Finished block: 6˝ × 6˝ • **Finished quilt:** 48˝ × 48˝

This quilt was inspired by the show **Infinite Variety: Three Centuries of Red and White Quilts**. *It reminds me of a bartender shaking a martini—hence the title. But if red is not your color, by all means choose another! Pick your favorite hue and then choose a background color that plays well with it. Do not feel limited to solids for this design; use variegated or tonal prints, or several different fabrics with the same color and value.*

Blue and white is another great option for this quilt. Darker blues in the border help frame the center of the quilt.

Cool colors and a light background create a wonderful option for a baby quilt.

Materials

White:
1⅞ yards

Red:
2 yards

Backing:
3⅛ yards

Batting:
56″ × 56″

Binding:
¾ yard red
(½″ finished width)

Cutting

To make templates for cutting, use Patterns 1 and 2 (page 78).

White

- Cut 3 strips 6½″ × width of fabric.

  Subcut into 16 squares 6½″ × 6½″.

  Subcut into frames using Template 2.

  From the quarter-circle waste fabric:

  Cut 16 squares 2½″ × 2½″.

- Cut 4 strips 5½″ × width of fabric.

  Subcut into 28 quarter-circles using Template 1.

- Cut 2 strips 2½″ × width of fabric.

  Subcut into 28 squares 2½″ × 2½″.

- Cut 2 strips 3½″ × 24½″.
- Cut 2 strips 3½″ × 30½″.

Red

- Cut 5 strips 6½″ × width of fabric.

  Subcut into 28 squares 6½″ × 6½″.

  Subcut into 28 frames using Template 2.

  From the quarter-circle waste fabric:

  Cut 28 squares 2½″ × 2½″.

- Cut 3 strips 5½″ × width of fabric.

  Subcut into 16 quarter-circles using Template 1 and 16 squares 2½″ × 2½″.

- Cut 2 strips 3½″ × 30½″.
- Cut 2 strips 3½″ × 36½″.

Backing

- Cut 2 pieces 56″ × width of fabric.

Binding

- Cut 6 strips 3½″ × width of fabric. (This is for a ½″ finished binding. If you prefer a narrower binding, adjust the cut strip size as desired.)

Construction

Seam allowances are ¼″. For detailed instructions on how to create this block, refer to Corner Triangle Variation (page 14).

Block Assembly

Block A

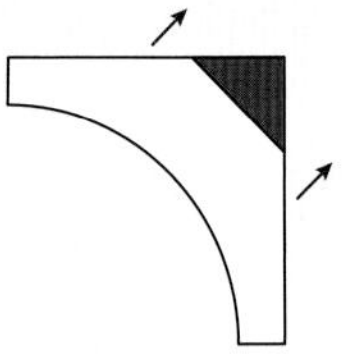
Make 16.

1. Sew 1 red square 2½″ × 2½″ onto 1 white frame piece to make a corner triangle. Press the seam toward the red.

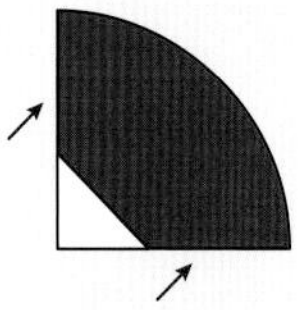
Make 16.

2. Sew 1 white square 2½″ × 2½″ onto 1 red quarter-circle piece to make a corner triangle. Press the seam toward the red.

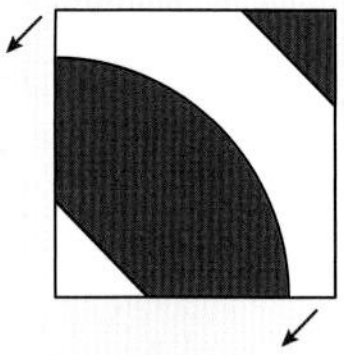
Make 16.

3. Sew together the 2 units made in Steps 1 and 2. Press the seam toward the red.

Quilt Construction

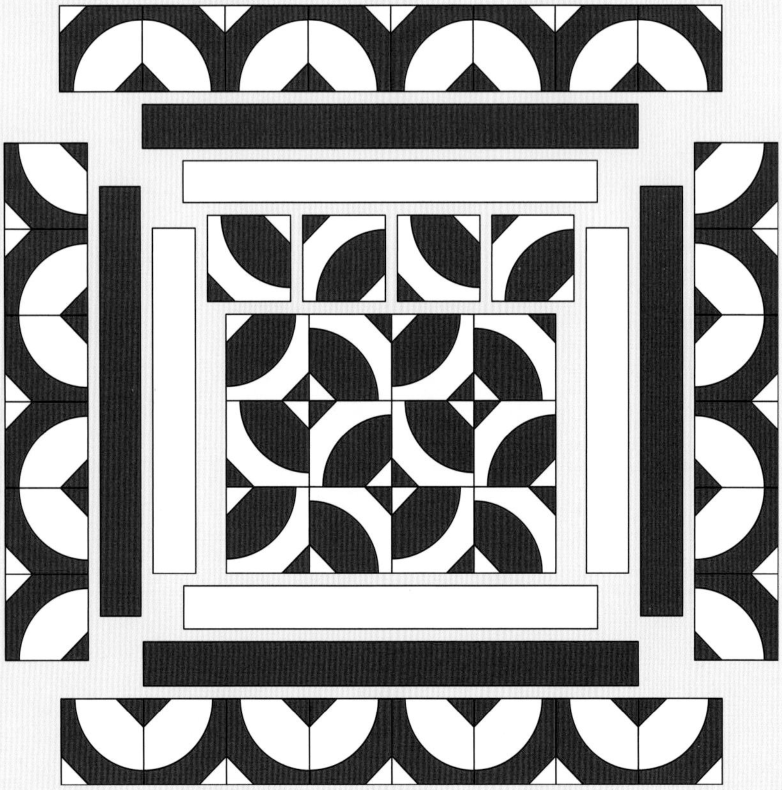
Shaken Not Stirred assembly

1. Arrange the blocks as shown in the *Shaken Not Stirred* assembly diagram.

2. Sew the blocks together into rows. Press the seams in opposite directions from row to row so that the seams nest.

3. Sew the rows together. Press the seams as you wish.

Borders

Inner Borders

1. Sew the 2 white strips 3½″ × 24½″ to the sides of the quilt. Press the seams toward the body of the quilt.

2. Sew the 2 white strips 3½″ × 30½″ to the top and bottom of the quilt. Press the seams toward the body of the quilt.

3. Sew the 2 red strips 3½″ × 30½″ to the sides of the quilt. Press the seams toward the red border.

4. Sew the 2 red strips 3½″ × 36½″ to the top and bottom of the quilt. Press the seams toward the red border.

Outer Borders

Block B

Make 28.

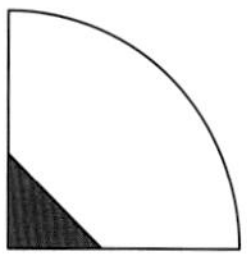

Make 28.

Make 28.

1. Sew 1 white square 2½″ × 2½″ onto 1 red frame piece to make a corner triangle. Wait to press the seams.

2. Sew 1 red square 2½″ × 2½″ onto 1 white quarter-circle piece to make a corner triangle. Wait to press the seams.

3. Sew together the units made in Steps 1 and 2. Wait to press the seams.

Outer Border Units

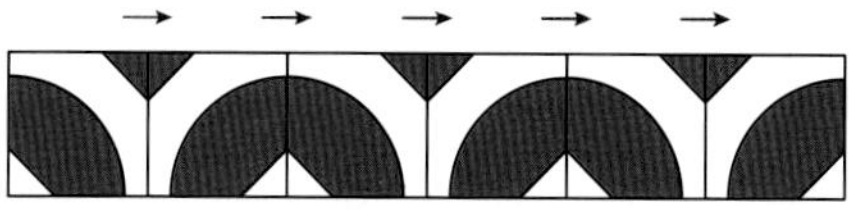

Make 4.

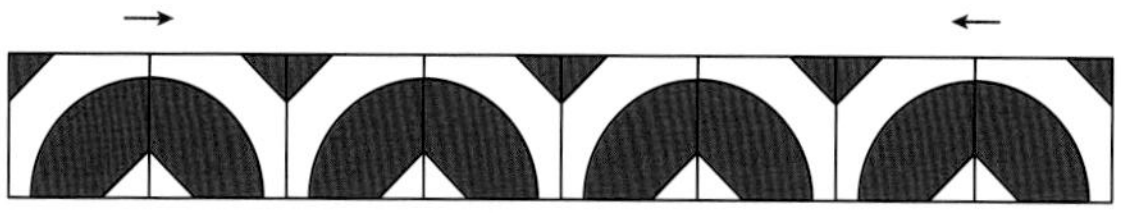

Make 2.

1. Sew together 6 Blocks B to create a border unit, pressing the seams so that they nest.

2. Sew 2 border units to the sides of the quilt. Press the seams toward the red inner border.

3. Sew 2 Blocks B to both ends of the remaining border units, pressing the seams so that they nest.

4. Sew the border units made in Step 3 to the top and bottom of the quilt. Press the seams toward the red inner border.

Finishing

1. Trim the selvage edges of the 2 backing pieces and sew them together along the 56″ sides.

2. Layer, baste, and quilt as desired.

3. Sew together the 3½″-wide binding strips on the diagonal.

4. Attach the binding to the quilt with a ½″ seam allowance using your preferred method.

MILLSTONES

Finished block: 8˝ × 8˝ • **Finished quilt:** 58˝ × 74˝

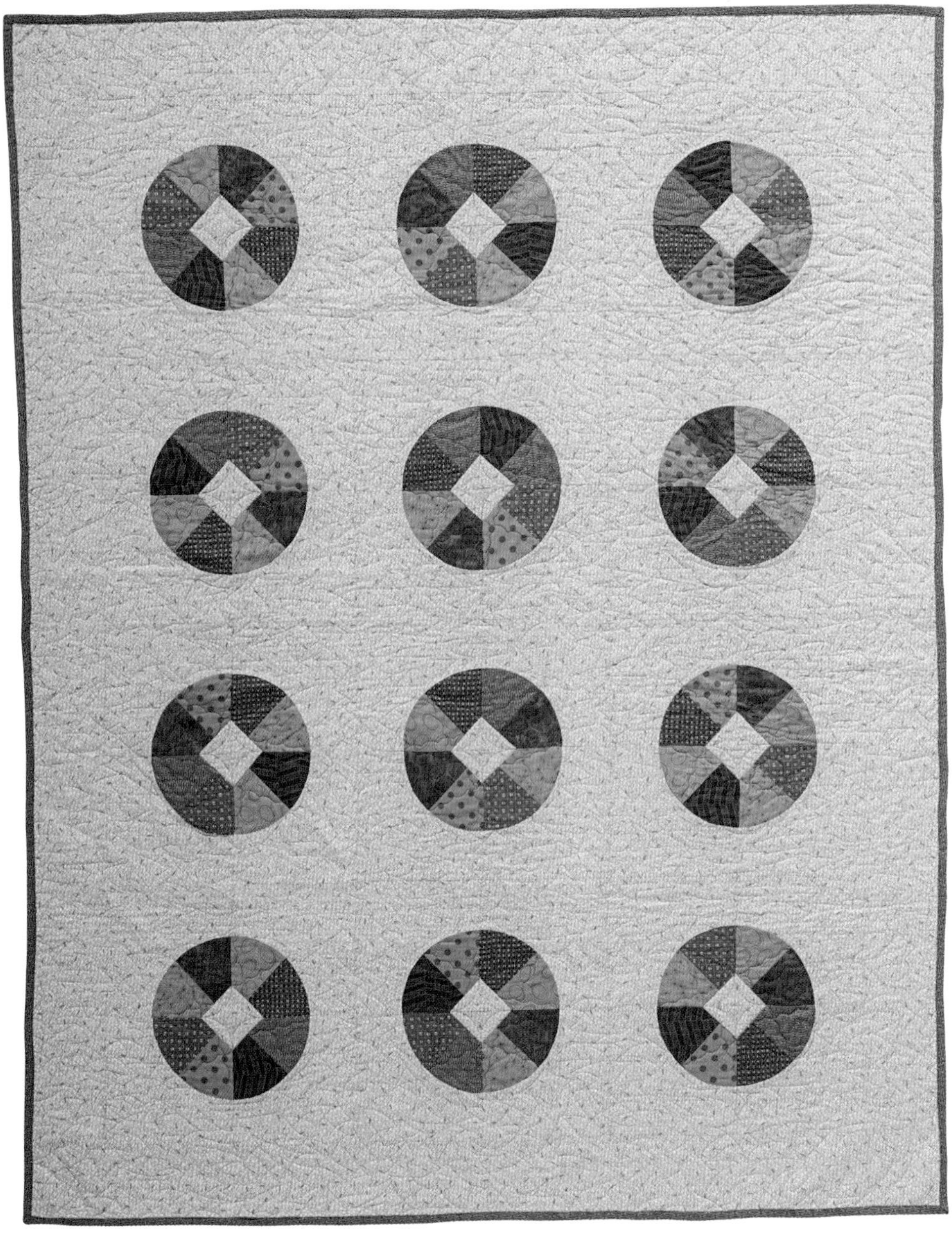

Tans and grays pulled from my stash help create the look of old millstones in this earthy quilt, but I could also see taking this design in a colorful direction. Medium-value colors or even bright primaries will work here; just choose a background that showcases whatever hues you have in the circles. ***Millstones*** *was designed without a border to create a floating effect, but by using a different color for the outer strips, you can give yours a frame.*

Adding a border gives *Millstones* a totally different look. This is the same design as the original, except that here the outer borders are cut from a tonal gray fabric instead of the background color.

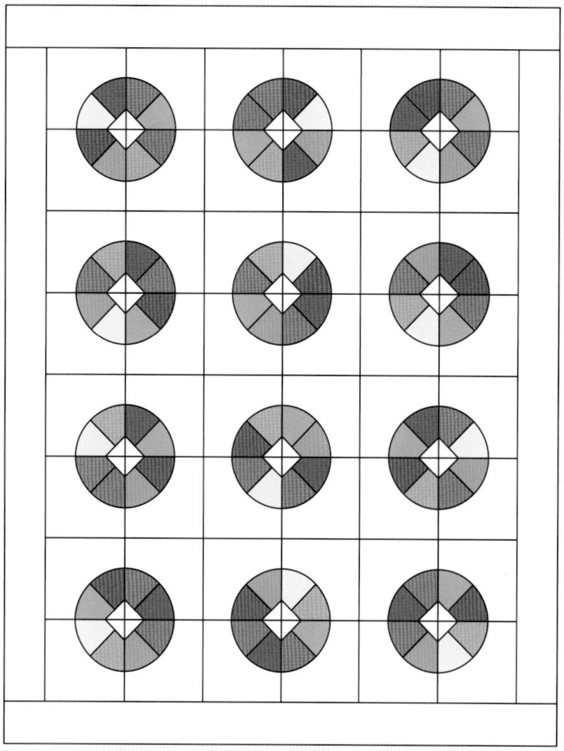

Create your own color wheels by using primary hues. Play with various colors and values in the different wheels.

Materials

These fabrics are tonal solids that resemble hand dyes; they have a subtle variation in color.

Assorted grays: 8 pieces, ⅓ yard of each

Cream: 4⅛ yards

Backing: 4⅝ yards

Batting: 66″ × 82″

Binding: 1 yard gray (½″ finished width)

Cutting

To make templates for cutting, use Patterns 1 and 2 (page 78).

Grays

- Cut 6 squares 6″ × 6″ from each fabric.

Cream

- Cut 8 strips 8½″ × width of fabric
  - Subcut into 32 squares 8½″ × 8½″.
    - Subcut into 32 frames using Template 2.
- Cut 2 strips parallel to the selvage 8½″ × 69″.
  - Subcut into 16 squares 8½″ × 8½″.
    - Subcut into 16 frames using Template 2.
      - *From the quarter-circle waste fabric:*
      - Subcut 48 squares 2½″ × 2½″.
- Cut 2 strips parallel to the selvage 5½″ × 64½″.
- Cut 2 strips parallel to the selvage 5½″ × 58½″.

Backing

- Cut 2 pieces 82″ × width of fabric.

Binding

- Cut 8 strips 3½″ × width of fabric. (This is for a ½″ finished binding. If you prefer a narrower binding, adjust accordingly.)

Construction

Seam allowances are ¼″. For detailed instructions on how to create this block, refer to Fan and Triangle Variation (page 16).

Block Assembly

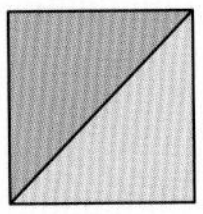

Make 48.

1. Sew together 2 different gray squares 6″ × 6″ along the diagonal to make 2 half-square triangle units. Press the seams as you wish. Trim the block to 5½″ × 5½″.

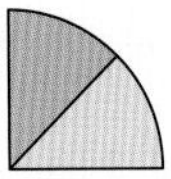

2. Subcut the half-square triangle units from Step 1 into quarter-circles using Template 1.

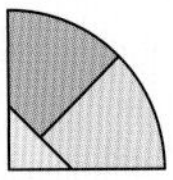

Make 48.

3. Sew 1 cream square 2½″ × 2½″ onto a unit from Step 2 to make a quarter-circle fan unit. Wait to press the seams.

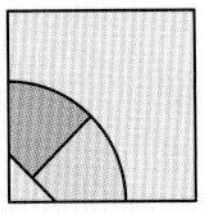

Make 48.

4. Sew together 1 cream frame unit and a quarter-circle fan unit. Wait to press the seams.

Quilt Construction

Millstones assembly

1. Arrange the blocks as shown in the *Millstones* assembly diagram. Reposition the blocks until you are pleased with the fabric placement. Press adjacent seams in opposite directions.

2. Sew the blocks together into rows. Press the seams in opposite directions from row to row so that the seams nest.

3. Sew the rows together. Press the seams as you wish.

Borders

1. Sew 2 strips 5½″ × 64½″ to the sides of the quilt. Press the seams toward the border.

2. Sew 2 strips 5½″ × 58½″ to the top and bottom of the quilt. Press the seams toward the border.

Finishing

1. Trim the selvage edges of the 2 backing pieces and join them together along the 82″ sides.

2. Layer, baste, and quilt as desired.

3. Sew the 3½″-wide binding strips together on the diagonal.

4. Attach the binding to the quilt with a ½″ seam allowance using your preferred method.

CHECKERBOARD

Finished block: 8″ × 8″ • **Finished quilt:** 64″ × 64″

Drunkard's Path blocks frame checkerboards in this high-contrast, graphic quilt made with **Peppered Cottons** *by Pepper Cory for Studio E Fabrics. This design is open to change, however. For another look, use 1930s reproduction fabrics—prints for the circles and solids for the backgrounds. Or pair tonal solids for the checkerboards and add a complimentary background.*

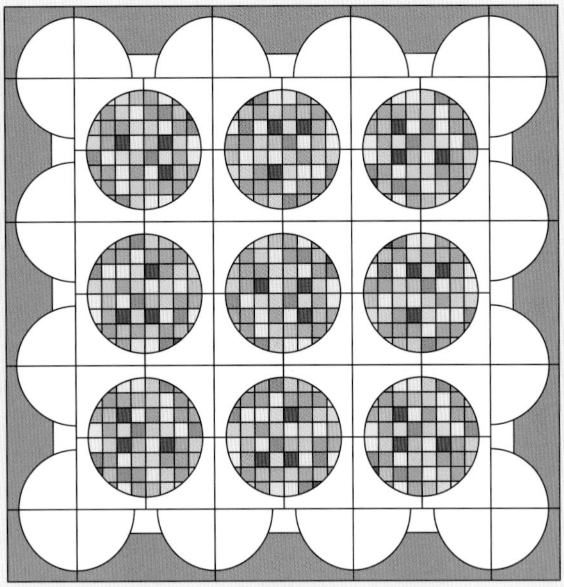

Colors reminiscent of 1930s reproduction prints give *Checkerboard* a cheerful look.

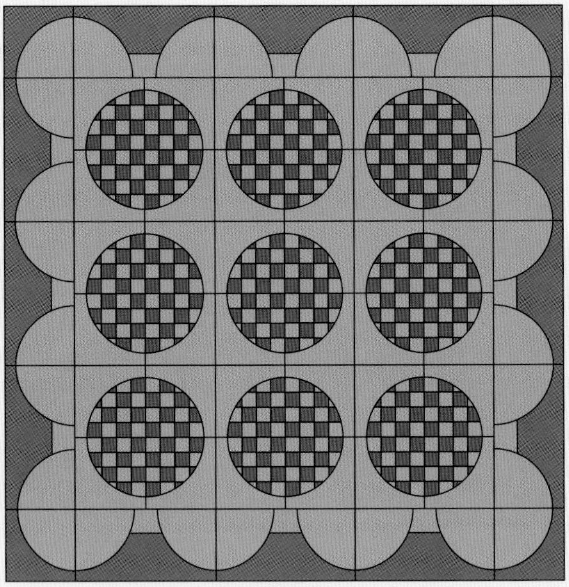

Replace the cream with gray and make the checkerboards from red and gray fabrics for a subtler look. The background works its way into the block, making the squares float.

DESIGN IDEA

Large-scale prints look totally different when they are cut up into smaller strips or squares. Try this technique to bring a great variety of color to your quilts. For the checkerboards, choose two large-scale prints, one dark and one light, for the strip sets.

Materials

Black: 1⅝ yards

Cream: 3½ yards

Medium-value solids: 8 pieces, ¼ yard or fat quarter of each

Dark-value solids: 8 pieces, ¼ yard or fat quarter of each

Backing: 4 yards

Batting: 72″ × 72″

Binding: 1 yard black (½″ finished width)

Cutting

To make templates for cutting, use Patterns 1 and 2 (page 78).

Black

- Cut 6 strips 6½″ × width of fabric.

  Subcut into 12 rectangles 6½″ × 16½″.

- Cut 1 strip 8½″ × width of fabric.

  Subcut into 4 squares 8½″ × 8½″.

  Subcut into 4 frames using Template 2.

Cream

- Cut 9 strips 8½″ × width of fabric.

  Subcut into 36 squares 8½″ × 8½″.

  Subcut into 36 frames using Template 2.

- Cut 6 strips 2½″ × width of fabric.

  Subcut into 12 rectangles 2½″ × 16½″.

- Cut 4 strips 5½″ × width of fabric.

  Subcut into 28 quarter-circles using Template 1.

Medium- and dark-value solids

From ¼-yard pieces:

- Cut 2 strips 1¾″ × width of fabric from each color; you will have 32 strips.

  Cut each strip in half widthwise, 1¾″ × approximately 20″.

From fat quarters:

- Cut 4 strips 1¾″ × 20″ from each fat quarter. You will have 64 strips.

Backing

- Cut 2 pieces 72″ × width of fabric.

Binding

- Cut 8 strips 3½″ × width of fabric. (This is for a ½″ finished binding. If you prefer a narrower binding, adjust accordingly.)

Construction

Seam allowances are ¼″. For detailed instructions on how to create this block, refer to Sixteen-Patch Variation (page 18).

Block Assembly

Make 16.

1. Randomly sew together 4 colored strips 1¾″ × 20″, alternating colors and values. Press the seams toward the darker fabric.

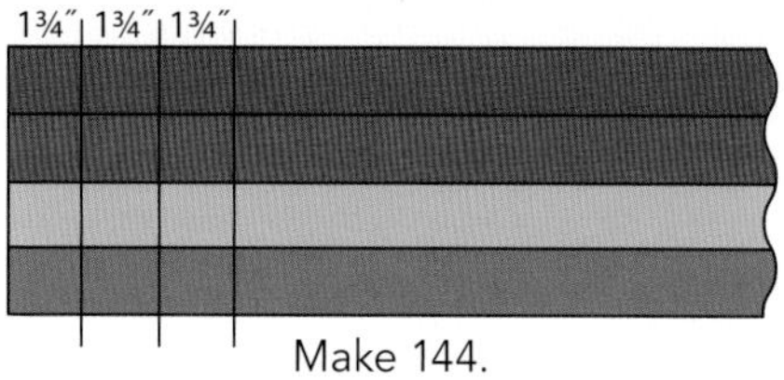

Make 144.

2. Subcut each strip set into rectangles 1¾″ × 5½″.

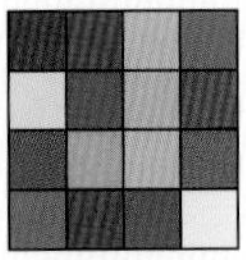
Make 36.

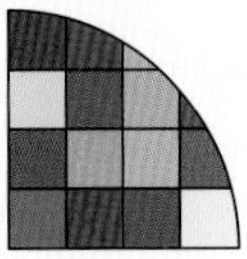
Make 36.

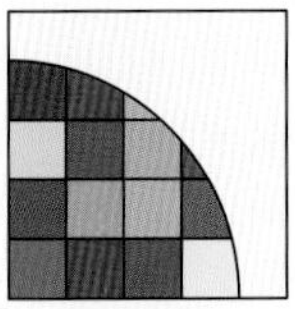
Make 36.

3. Randomly sew together 4 rectangles from Step 2 to create a Sixteen-Patch block. Press the seams open.

4. Subcut the blocks from Step 3 into quarter-circles using Template 1.

5. Sew together a cream frame and a Step 4 quarter-circle unit. Wait to press the seam.

Quilt Construction

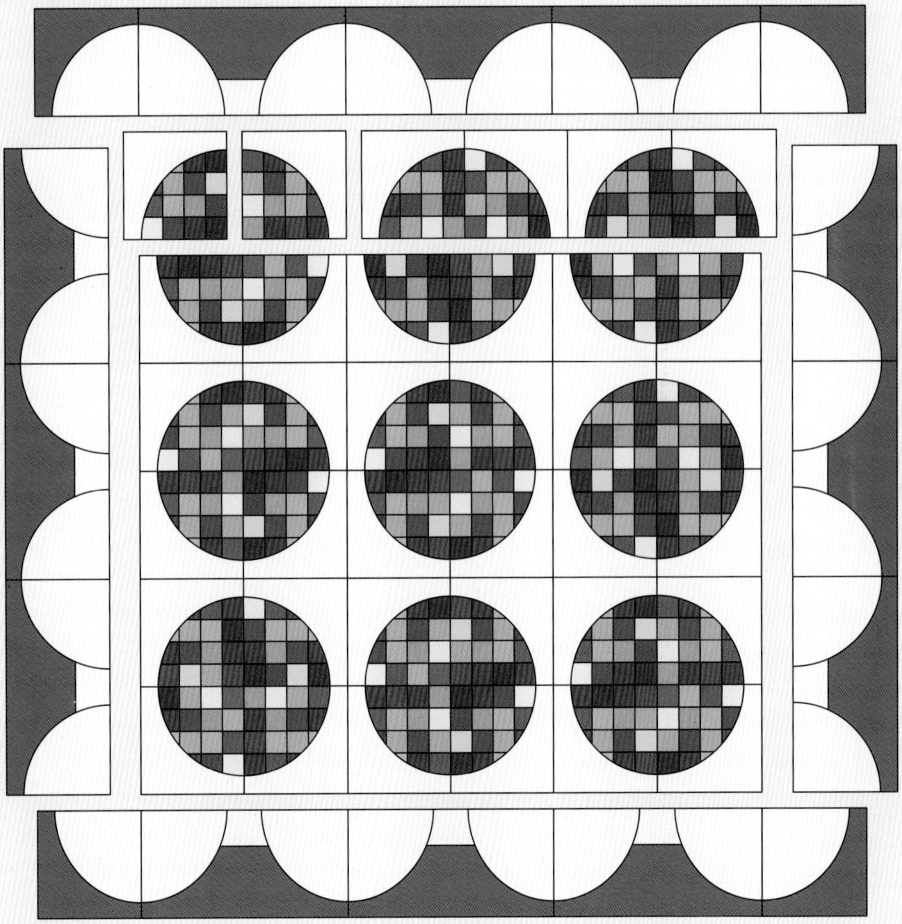
Checkerboard assembly

1. Arrange the blocks as shown in the *Checkerboard* assembly diagram. Reposition the blocks until you are pleased with the fabric placement. Press adjacent seams in opposite directions.

2. Sew the blocks together into rows. Press the seams in opposite directions from row to row so that the seams nest.

3. Sew the rows together. Press the seams toward the bottom of the quilt.

Borders

Border Units

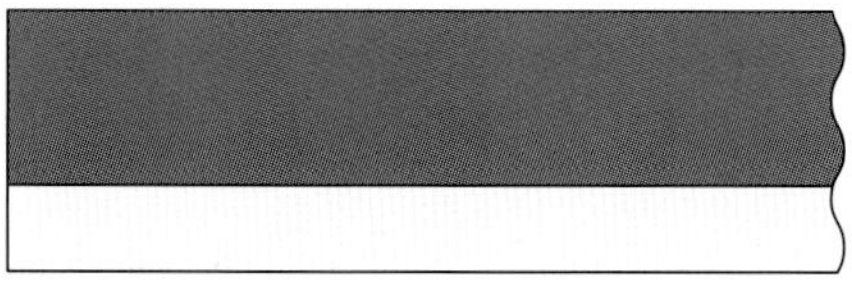

Make 12.

Make 12.

1. Sew a black strip 6½″ × 16½″ to a cream strip 2½″ × 16½″. Press open the seams.

2. Subcut the units from Step 1 into frames using Template 2.

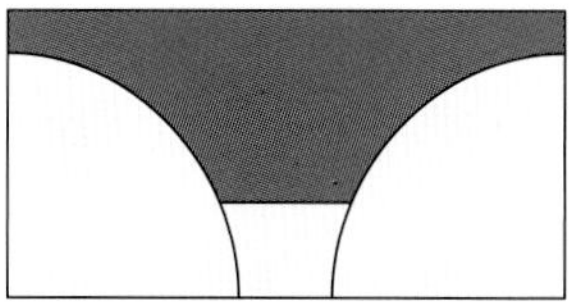

Make 12.

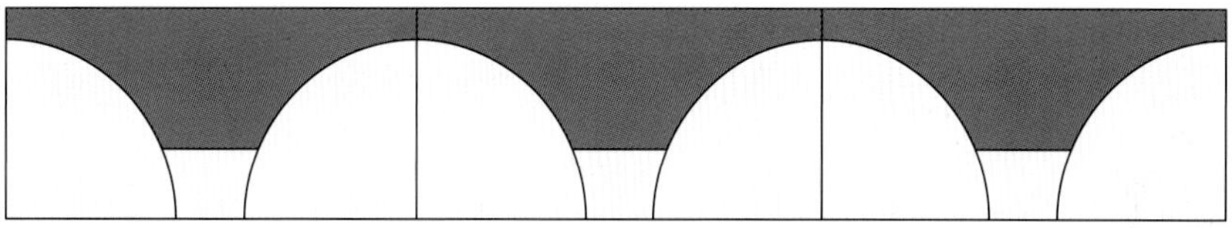

Make 4.

3. Sew 2 cream quarter-circles to the unit from Step 2 and press the seams open.

4. Sew together 3 units to create a border unit.

5. Sew a border unit to each side of the quilt. Press the seams toward the body of the quilt.

Corner Border Blocks

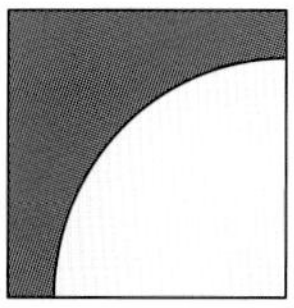

Make 4.

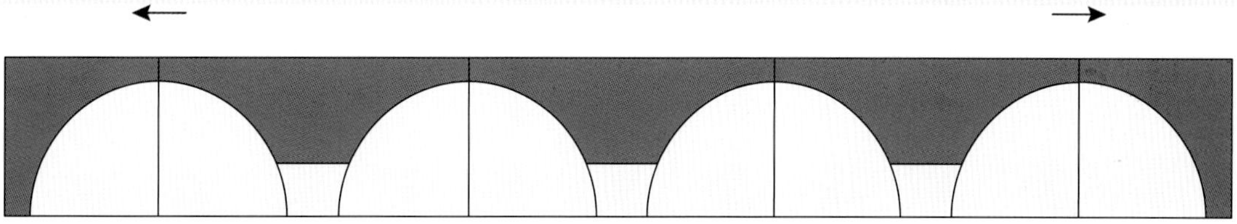

Make 2.

1. Sew together 1 cream quarter-circle unit and 1 black 8½″ × 8½″ frame unit to make a corner unit. Press open the seams.

2. Sew a corner unit to each end of the remaining border units and press the seams toward the corner unit. Sew the border units to the top and bottom of the quilt.

Finishing

1. Trim the selvage edges of the 2 backing pieces and join together along the 72″ sides.

2. Layer, baste, and quilt as desired.

3. Sew the 3½″-wide binding strips together on the diagonal.

4. Attach the binding to the quilt with a ½″ seam allowance using your preferred method.

PEACOCK ALLEY

Finished blocks: 6˝ × 6˝, 6˝ × 7˝, 7˝ × 7˝, 12˝ × 7˝ • **Finished quilt:** 62˝ × 62˝

Using the blocks as border treatments shifts the focus in this medallion quilt, which features Sarah Fielke's line **Enchanted** *for Windham Fabrics. When designing your own Peacock Alley, begin with a focus fabric for the central square and pick out the remaining fabrics based on the colors and images in your focus fabric.*

Swap the darks and lights to take your Peacock Alley to a different neighborhood.

An orphaned block looks right at home when framed by strong borders.

DESIGNER'S TIP

If your focus fabric is darker in value than what I used for Peacock Alley, *you can still use it in this design by swapping dark for light (and vice versa) throughout the quilt. Make the light values in your quilt dark values and the dark values light.*

DESIGNER'S TIP

Send your orphaned blocks over to Peacock Alley, where they will find a home! Do you have a complex block from a workshop sitting around? Or how about an appliquéd block that led you to decide you would never do appliqué again? This quilt design is the perfect place to use a block you already made but aren't sure how to use because the Drunkard's Path blocks function like a frame. So give that orphaned block an extra-special setting.

Materials

Focus fabric: 1⅓ yards

Magenta: ⅛ yard

White: 2½ yards

Yellow medium-scale print: ⅝ yard

Small-scale floral print: ¾ yard

Yellow-and-white stripe: ¾ yard

Small-scale green print: ⅝ yard

Backing: 4 yards

Batting: 70″ × 70″

Binding: 1 yard magenta (½″ finished width)

Cutting

Focus fabric

Consider the pattern in your focus print when cutting out the center square; you may want to center a design.

- Cut 1 square 18½″ × 18½″ for the central medallion.
- Cut 5 strips 5½″ × width of fabric.

  Subcut into 32 quarter-circles using Template 1.

Magenta

- Cut 2 strips 1½″ × width of fabric.

  Subcut into 2 strips 1½″ × 18½″ and 2 strips 1½″ × 20½″.

White

- Cut 4 strips 2½″ × width of fabric.

  Subcut into 2 strips 2½″ × 20½″ and 2 strips 2½″ × 24½″.
- Cut 4 strips 6½″ × width of fabric.

  Subcut into 20 squares 6½″ × 6½″.

    Subcut into 20 frames using Template 2.
- Cut 6 strips 2½″ × width of fabric.
- Cut 8 strips 3½″ × width of fabric.

  Subcut 2 strips into 4 rectangles 3½″ × 7½″, 4 rectangles 3½″ × 4½″, and 4 squares 2½″ × 2½″.

Yellow medium-scale print

- Cut 3 strips 5½″ × width of fabric.

  Subcut into 20 quarter-circles using Template 1.

Small-scale floral print

- Cut 2 strips 2½″ × width of fabric.

  Subcut into 20 squares 2½″ × 2½″.
- Cut 5 strips 3½″ × width of fabric.

  Subcut into 2 rectangles 3½″ × 36½″.

Yellow-and-white stripe

- Cut 6 strips 3½″ × width of fabric.

Small-scale green print

- Cut 7 strips 2½″ × width of fabric.

  Subcut 1 strip into 4 squares 2½″ × 2½″ and 4 rectangles 2½″ × 4½″.

Backing

- Cut 2 pieces 70″ × width of fabric.

Binding

- Cut 7 magenta strips 3½″ × width of fabric. (This is for a ½″ finished binding. If you prefer a narrower binding, adjust accordingly.)

Construction

Seam allowances are ¼″. Refer to the Peacock Alley *assembly diagram.*

Peacock Alley assembly

Central Medallion

1. Sew 2 magenta strips 1½″ × 18½″ to the sides of the central medallion square. Press the seams toward the magenta.

2. Sew 2 magenta strips 1½″ × 20½″ to the top and bottom of the central medallion unit. Press the seams toward the magenta.

3. Sew 2 white strips 2½″ × 20½″ to the sides of the central medallion unit. Press the seams toward the magenta.

4. Sew 2 white strips 2½″ × 24½″ to the top and bottom of the central medallion unit. Press toward the magenta.

Pieced Inner Border

For detailed instructions on how to create this block, refer to Corner Triangle Variation (page 14).

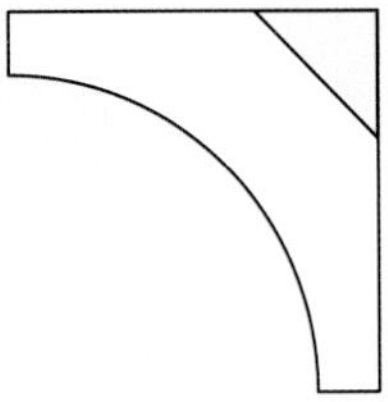

Make 20.

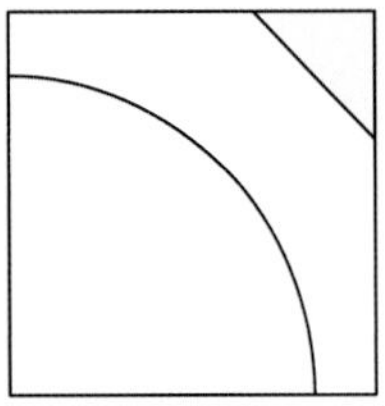

Make 20.

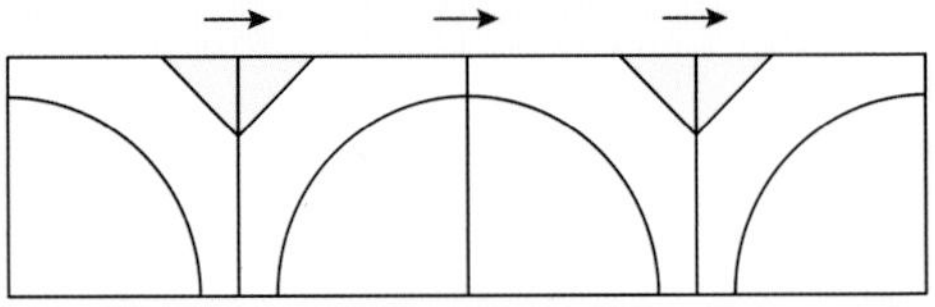

Make 4.

1. Sew a small-scale floral print square 2½″ × 2½″ to a white frame piece, making a corner triangle. Press open the seam.

2. Sew a yellow-print quarter-circle unit to a frame unit from Step 1. Wait to press the seam.

3. Sew together 4 units from Step 2, pressing the seams between the blocks as you go so they will nest. Press the seams in the completed row to the right.

4. Sew a border strip from Step 3 to each side of the quilt. Press the seams toward the white inner border.

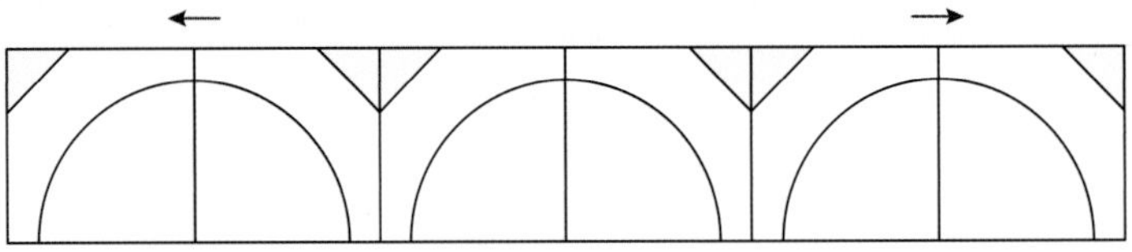

Make 2.

5. Sew 2 blocks to the ends of each remaining Step 3 unit. Press the seams toward the corner end blocks.

6. Attach the border strips from Step 5 to the top and bottom of the quilt. Press the seams toward the pieced inner border.

Small-Scale Floral Print Inner Border

1. Sew 2 small-scale floral print strips 3½″ × 36½″ to the sides of the quilt. Press the seams toward the floral print border.

2. Stitch together the 3 remaining floral print strips diagonally and subcut into 2 strips 3½″ × 42½″. Sew these borders to the top and bottom of the quilt. Press the seams toward the floral print border.

DESIGNER'S TIP

If you are not using a striped fabric for this border, you can omit the mitered corners. After sewing the strips together, cut 2 strips 3½″ × 42½″ for the side borders and 2 strips 3½″ × 48½″ for the top and bottom borders.

Yellow-and-White Stripe Inner Border

1. Stitch the yellow-and-white stripe strips together on the diagonal and subcut into 4 strips 3½″ × 54½″.

2. Attach the strips from Step 1 to all 4 sides of the quilt following the instructions for Mitered Corners (next page). Press the seams toward the floral border.

Mitered Corners

1. Place a pin at the center points of all 4 border strips that will be attached to the quilt with a mitered corner. Measure from this center point one-half of the width of the quilt (this quilt is 42½″, so one-half would be 21¼″) and mark with another pin. Measure from the center to the opposite end and mark with another pin. Repeat for the 3 remaining borders.

2. Mark the center points of all 4 sides of the quilt with a pin.

3. Pin the side border strips to the quilt top, matching the center points and the marked length on the borders to the edges of the quilt top.

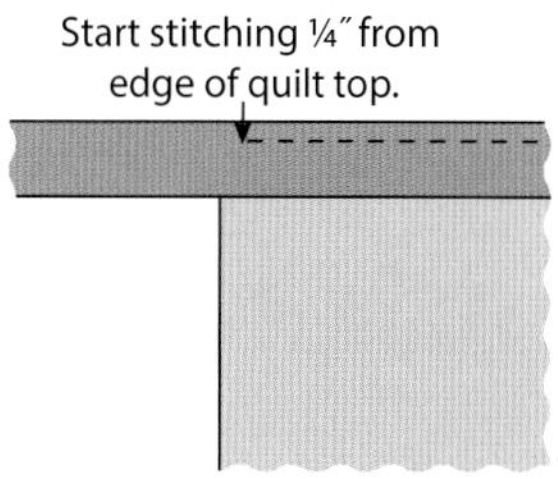

Stop stitching ¼″ from the edge.

4. Stitch the strips to the sides of the quilt top by starting ¼″ in from the beginning edge of the quilt top. Stitch forward ¼″, then backstitch ¼″, and then continue forward down the length of the side border. Stop stitching ¼″ before the ending edge of the quilt top, at the seam allowance line, and backstitch. Press the seams toward the borders.

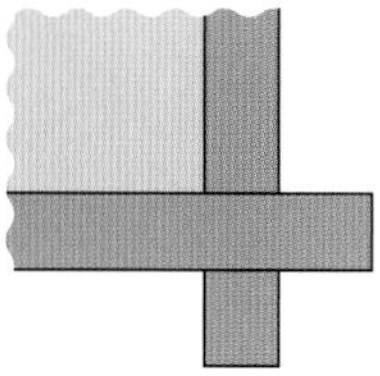
Border strip on top of an adjacent strip

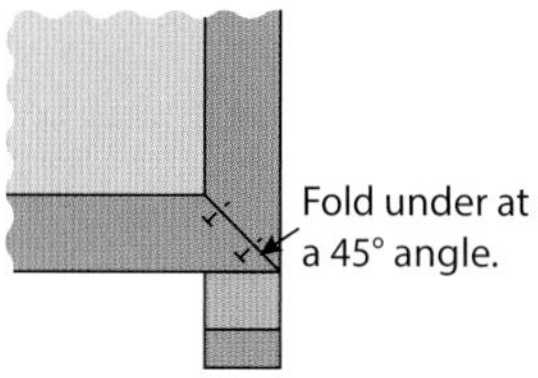

Fold under at a 45° angle.

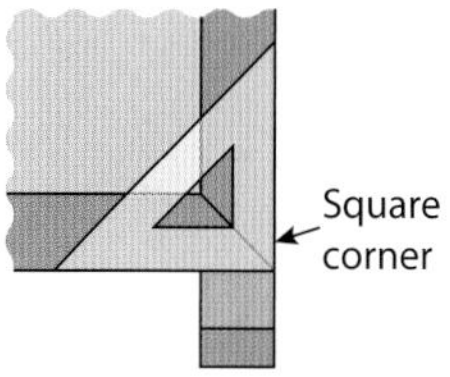

Square corner

5. Repeat for the top and bottom borders.

6. Lay the quilt, right side up, on an ironing board and place 1 border strip on top of the adjacent border.

7. With right sides up, fold the top border strip under itself so that it meets the edge of the adjacent border and forms a 45° angle. Pin the fold in place.

8. Position a right triangle or ruler over the corner to check that the corner is flat and square. When everything is in place, press the fold firmly.

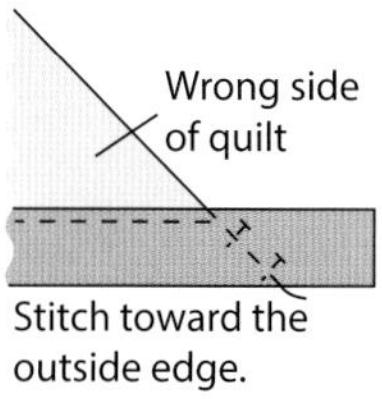

Stitch the mitered corner.

9. Remove the pins. Fold the center section of the top diagonally from the corner, right sides together, and align the long edges of the border strips. On the wrong side, place pins near the pressed fold in the corner to secure the border strips.

10. Beginning at the inside corner at the border seamline, stitch, backstitch, and then stitch along the fold toward the outside point of the border corners. Backstitch at the end. Check that the seam is correct and that the corner lies flat, and then trim the excess border fabric to a ¼″ seam allowance. Press the seam open.

11. Repeat Steps 6–10 for the 3 other corners.

Pieced Outer Border

Make Strip Sets

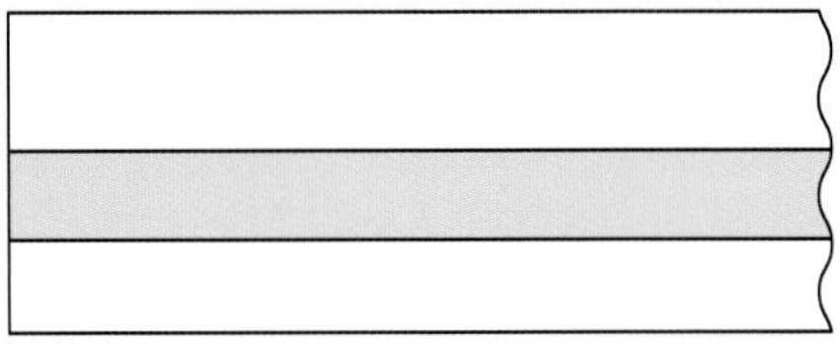

Make 6.

1. Sew 1 white strip 2½″ × width of fabric and 1 white strip 3½″ × width of fabric to either side of 1 green print strip 2½″ × width of fabric. Press the seams open.

2. Subcut the strip sets from Step 1 into 12 rectangles 7½″ × 12½″ and 8 rectangles 7½″ × 6½″.

Border Blocks

Refer to Rail Fence Variation (page 18) and Corner Triangle Variation (page 14) for detailed instructions on how to create this block.

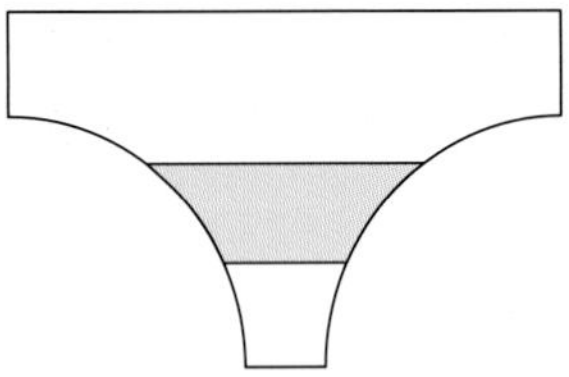

Make 12.

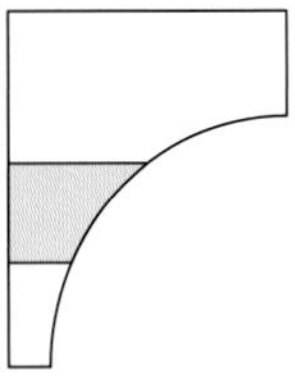

Make 4.

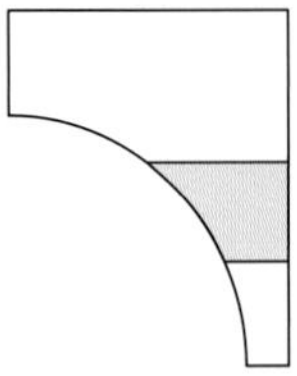

Make 4.

1. Subcut the 12 strip-set rectangles 7½″ × 12½″ into 12 frames using Template 2.

2. Subcut 4 strip-set rectangles 7½″ × 6½″ into 4 frames using Template 2 with a left orientation as shown.

3. Subcut 4 strip-set rectangles 7½″ × 6½″ into 4 frames using Template 2 with a right orientation as shown.

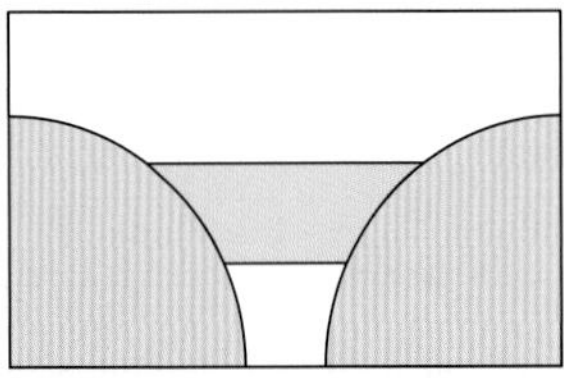

Block A: Make 12.

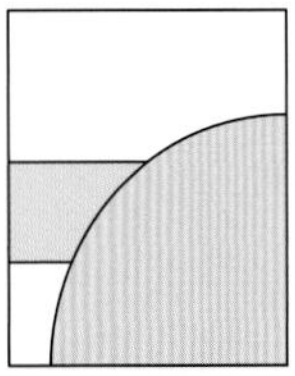

Block B1: Make 4.

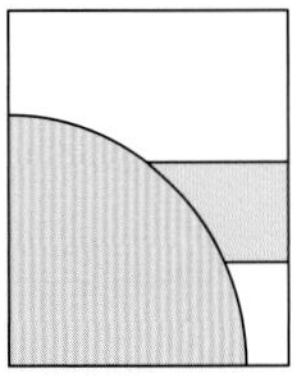

Block B2: Make 4.

4. Sew a quarter-circle of focus fabric to each of the frame units made in Steps 1–3 to make Blocks A, B1, and B2 as shown. Wait to press the seams.

Corner Border Block

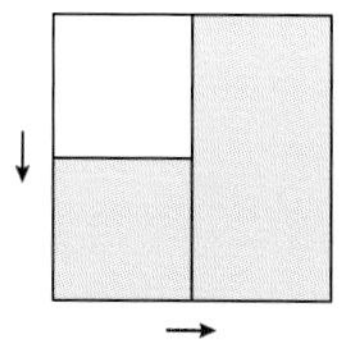

Make 4.

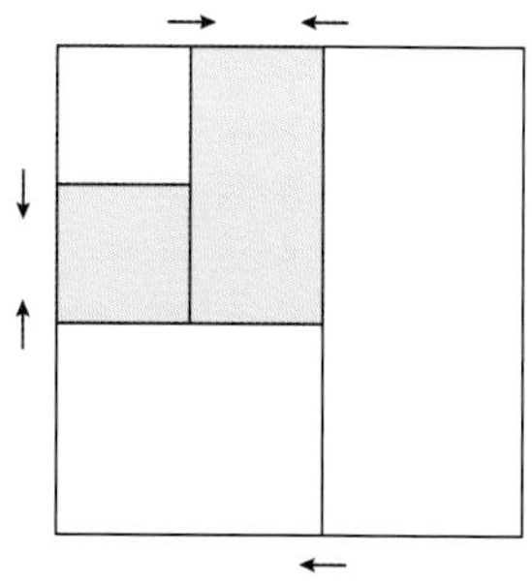

Make 4.

1. Sew a white square 2½″ × 2½″ to a green print square 2½″ × 2½″. Press the seam toward the green. Sew a green print rectangle 2½″ × 4½″ to the unit just created. Press the seam toward the green unit.

2. Sew a white rectangle 3½″ × 4½″ to the unit from Step 1. Press the seam toward the green. Sew a white piece 3½″ × 7½″ to the unit just created. Press the seam toward the green.

Border Units

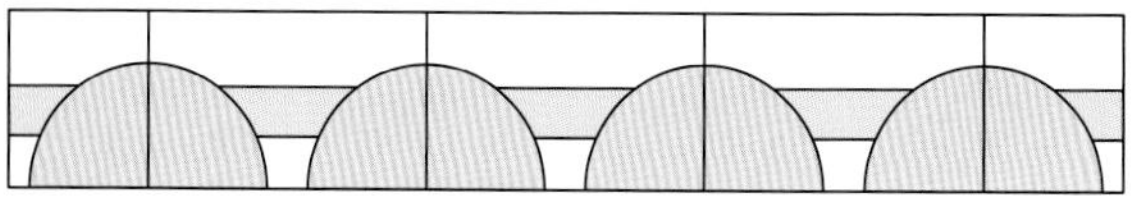

Make 4.

1. Sew together 3 Blocks A and 1 each of Blocks B1 and B2 to make an outer border strip. Press the seams as you go so that they nest. Press the seams in a finished row as you wish.

2. Sew 2 outer border strips to the sides of the quilt. Press the seams toward the inner border.

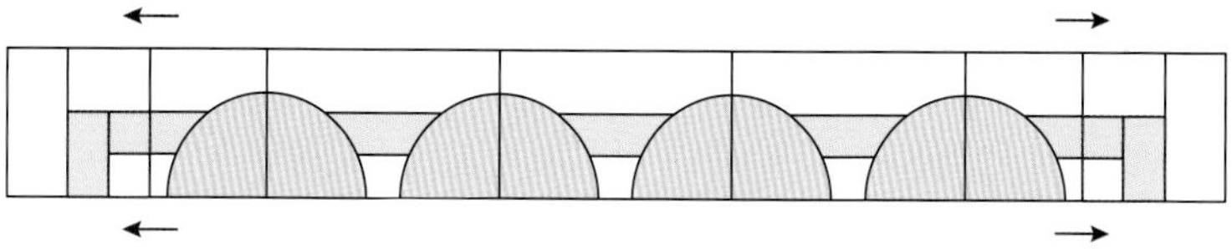

Make 2.

3. Sew 2 corner border blocks to the ends of the remaining outer border strips. Press the seams toward the corner blocks.

4. Sew the remaining outer border strips to the top and bottom of the quilt. Press the seams toward the inner border.

Finishing

1. Trim the selvage edges of the 2 backing pieces and join them together along the 70″ sides.

2. Layer, baste, and quilt as desired.

3. Sew together the 3½″-wide binding strips on the diagonal.

4. Attach the binding to the quilt with a ½″ seam allowance using your preferred method.

TEMPLATES

Follow instructions for Making Templates 101 (page 10).

1″ × 1″
Size
Verification

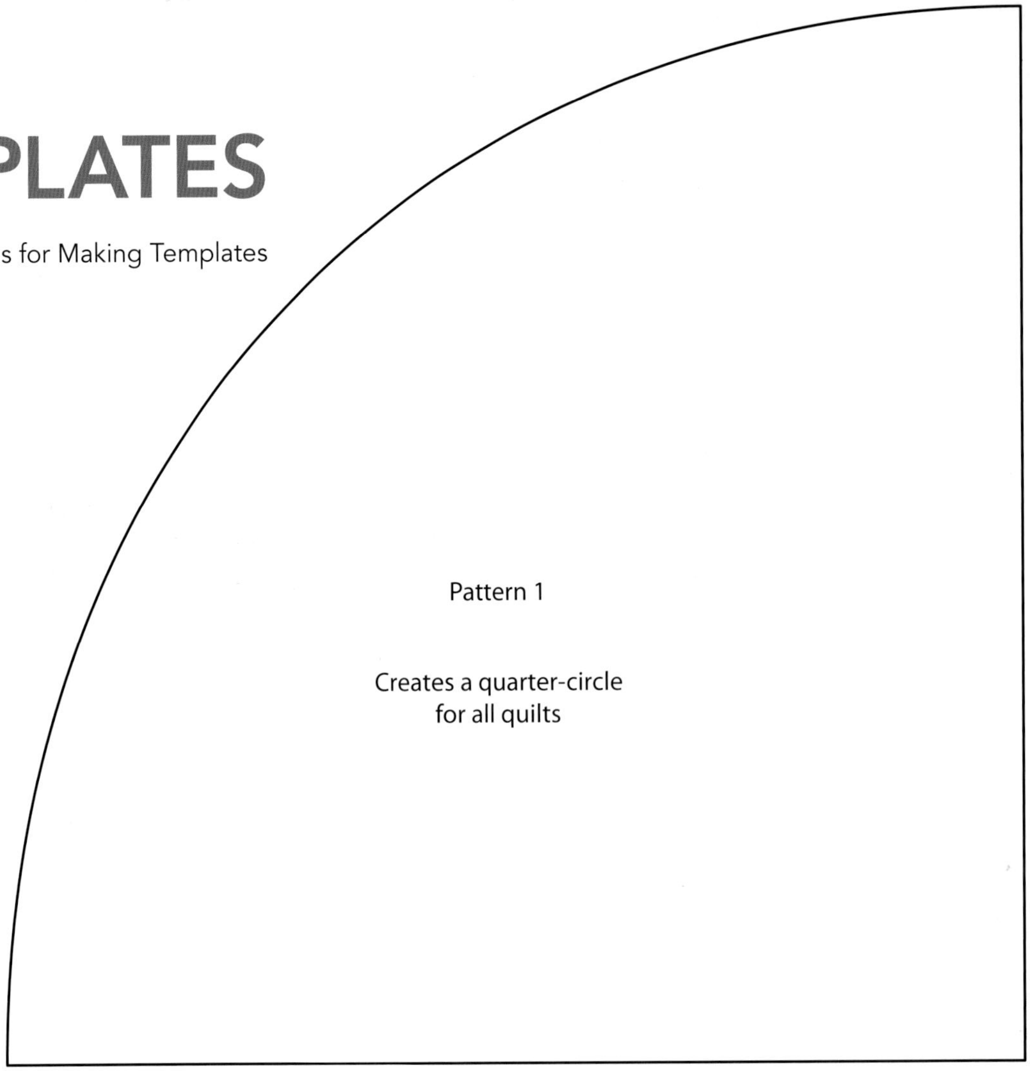

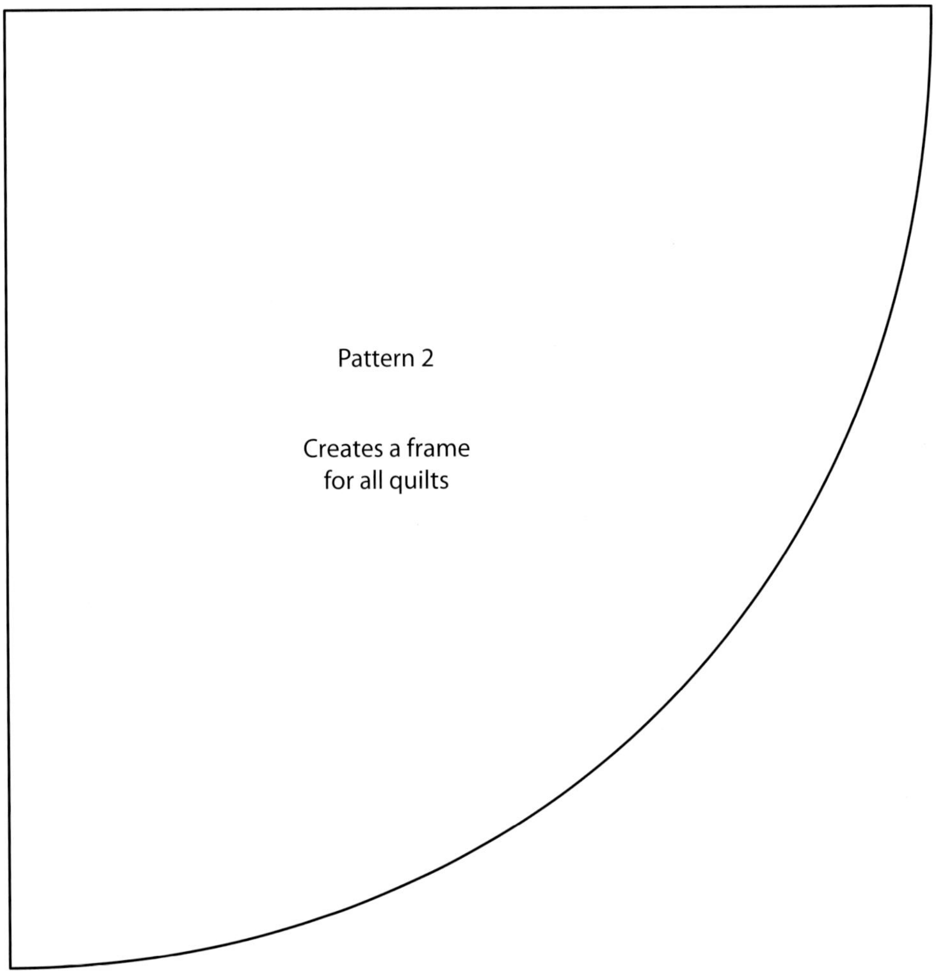

about THE AUTHOR

John Kubiniec has been crafty all his life. Growing up, John was surrounded by makers—his father was a woodworker, and his mother and sisters were always making things, from braided rugs and knit sweaters to macramé owls and pottery. Over the years, John dabbled in woodworking, candle making, cross-stitch, embroidery, leatherwork, and crocheting. He was getting serious with ceramics before he found quilting in 1999.

He was a runner-up in the 2010 McCall's Design Star Competition. His quilt patterns have appeared in *McCall's Quilting, McCall's Quick Quilts, Fat Quarterly,* and Fons & Porter's *Easy Quilts.* He has designed patterns for Windham Fabrics, RJR Fabrics, and Red Rooster. John was one of the panelists at the American Folk Art Museum's program *Quiltmakers: Real Men Quilt* in June 2011 and his HQ Story was chosen for Handi Quilter's 2012 ad campaign. He is a BERNINA Brand Ambassador and served as a tester in the development of the BERNINA Q 24 and Q 20 longarm machines.

Want even more creative content?
Go to ctpub.com/offer
& sign up to receive our gift to you!
MENU
C&T PUBLISHING
Your Home for Creative Quilting & Sewing
HAND PRINTING STUDIO
Print on Almost Anything!
Get some in-spiration
GET INSPIRED
GARMENT SEWING LOOKBOOK 2016
Make it, snap it, share it
using
#ctpublishing
59
58